COMMON CORE
LANGUAGE
ARTS
4 Today

**Daily
Skill Practice**

Grade 2

Carson-Dellosa Publishing, LLC
Greensboro, North Carolina

Credits

Content Editor: Christine Schwab
Copy Editor: Julie B. Killian

 Visit *carsondellosa.com* for correlations to Common Core State, national, and Canadian provincial standards.

Carson-Dellosa Publishing, LLC
PO Box 35665
Greensboro, NC 27425 USA
carsondellosa.com

ISBN 978-1-62442-605-6

Table of Contents

Common Core Language Arts 4 Today: Daily Skill Practice is a perfect supplement to any classroom language arts curriculum. Students' reading skills will grow as they work on comprehension, fluency, vocabulary, and decoding. Students' writing skills will improve as they work on elements of writing, writing structure, genre, parts of speech, grammar, and spelling, as well as the writing process.

This book covers 40 weeks of daily practice. Four comprehension questions or writing exercises a day for four days a week will provide students with ample practice in language arts skills. A separate assessment is included for the fifth day of each week.

Various skills and concepts are reinforced throughout the book through activities that align to the Common Core State Standards. To view these standards, please see the Common Core State Standards Alignment Matrix on pages 7 and 8.

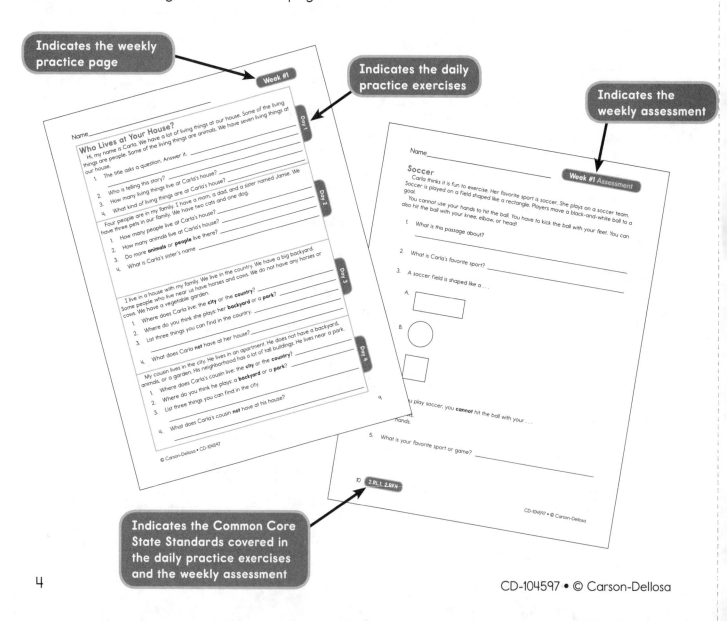

Indicates the weekly practice page

Indicates the daily practice exercises

Indicates the weekly assessment

Indicates the Common Core State Standards covered in the daily practice exercises and the weekly assessment

Building a Reading Environment

A positive reading environment is essential to fostering successful readers. When building a reading environment, think of students' physical, emotional, and cognitive needs.

Physical Environment
- Make the physical reading environment inviting and comfortable. Create a reading corner with comfortable chairs, floor pillows, a rug, enticing lighting, etc.
- Give students access to a variety of texts by providing books, magazines, newspapers, and Internet access. Read signs, ads, posters, menus, pamphlets, labels, boxes, and more!
- Provide regularly scheduled independent reading time in class. Encourage students to read at home. They can read to a younger sibling or read anything of interest such as comic books, children's and sports magazines, chapter books, etc.
- Set a positive example. Make sure students see you reading too!

Emotional Environment
- Learn about students' reading habits, preferences, strengths, and weaknesses. Then, provide books that address these issues.
- Help students create connections with text. Facilitate connections by activating prior knowledge, examining personal meaning, and respecting personal reflections.
- Give students the opportunity to choose titles to read. This will give them a sense of ownership, which will engage them in the text and sustain interest.
- Create a safe environment for exploring and trying new things. Foster a feeling of mutual respect for reading abilities and preferences.
- Require students to read at an appropriate reading level. Text in any content area, including leisure reading, should not be too easy or too difficult.
- Have all students participate in reading, regardless of their reading levels. Try to include slower readers and be sure to give them time to finish before moving on or asking questions.
- Be enthusiastic about reading! Talk about books you love and share your reading experiences and habits. Your attitude about reading is contagious!

Cognitive Environment
- Regardless of the grade level, read aloud to students every day. Reading aloud not only provides a good example but also lets students practice their listening skills.
- Help students build their vocabularies to make their reading more successful. Create word walls, personal word lists, mini-dictionaries, and graphic organizers.
- Read for different purposes. Reading a novel requires different skills than reading an instruction manual. Teach students the strategies needed to comprehend these different texts.
- Encourage students to talk about what and how they read. Use journal writing, literature circles, class discussions, conferences, conversations, workshops, seminars, and more.
- Writing and reading are inherently linked. Students can examine their own writing through reading and examine their reading skills by writing. Whenever possible, facilitate the link between reading and writing.

Writing Strategies

Choose a **topic** for your writing.
- What am I writing about?

Decide on a **purpose** for writing.
- Why am I writing this piece?
- What do I hope the audience will learn from reading this piece?

Identify your **audience**.
- Who am I writing to?

Decide on a writing **style**.
- Expository—gives information or explains facts or ideas
- Persuasive—tries to talk someone into something
- Narrative—tells a story
- Descriptive—presents a clear picture of a person, place, thing, or idea

Decide on a **genre**—essay, letter, poetry, autobiography, fiction, or nonfiction.

Decide on a **point of view**—first person, second person, or third person.

Brainstorm by listing or drawing your main ideas.

Use a graphic organizer to **organize** your thoughts.

Revise, revise, revise!
- Use **descriptive words**.
- Use **transitions** and linking expressions.
- Use a **variety of sentence structures**.
- **Elaborate** with facts and details.
- Group your ideas into **paragraphs**.
- **Proofread** for capitalization, punctuation, and spelling.

Common Core State Standards Alignment Matrix

STANDARD	W1	W2	W3	W4	W5	W6	W7	W8	W9	W10	W11	W12	W13	W14	W15	W16	W17	W18	W19	W20
2.RL.1	●		●				●		●		●		●		●				●	
2.RL.2																			●	
2.RL.3					●	●														
2.RL.4				●			●		●	●			●							
2.RL.5																		●		
2.RL.6															●					
2.RL.7																				
2.RL.9											●				●					
2.RL.10			●																	
2.RI.1					●		●		●				●		●		●			
2.RI.2					●								●		●		●			
2.RI.3																		●		
2.RI.4			●		●				●											
2.RI.5					●															
2.RI.6					●				●						●					
2.RI.7						●				●		●				●		●		
2.RI.8																		●		
2.RI.9					●															
2.RI.10					●		●		●				●		●		●			
2.RF.3		●	●					●	●					●	●					
2.RF.4	●				●		●		●		●		●		●		●		●	
2.W.1											●	●	●			●				
2.W.2					●															
2.W.3																				
2.W.5				●		●				●			●			●		●		
2.W.6						●				●			●			●		●		
2.W.7													●			●				
2.W.8				●							●									
2.L.1					●	●	●			●			●		●			●		●
2.L.2		●		●		●		●	●	●			●		●			●		●
2.L.3		●	●	●		●		●		●			●		●			●		●
2.L.4			●		●				●						●					
2.L.5			●													●				
2.L.6					●		●				●									

W = Week

Common Core State Standards Alignment Matrix

STANDARD	W21	W22	W23	W24	W25	W26	W27	W28	W29	W30	W31	W32	W33	W34	W35	W36	W37	W38	W39	W40
2.RL.1	●			●			●		●		●	●	●				●		●	
2.RL.2									●											
2.RL.3	●						●				●									
2.RL.4			●										●							
2.RL.5																	●			
2.RL.6																			●	
2.RL.7				●																
2.RL.9																				
2.RL.10													●							
2.RI.1			●	●	●		●					●			●				●	
2.RI.2							●								●					
2.RI.3																				
2.RI.4					●										●				●	
2.RI.5																				
2.RI.6																				
2.RI.7		●		●				●								●		●		
2.RI.8																				
2.RI.9															●					
2.RI.10			●		●		●								●				●	
2.RF.3	●				●				●	●					●				●	
2.RF.4			●		●	●	●		●		●	●	●	●	●		●		●	
2.W.1												●						●		
2.W.2		●													●					
2.W.3							●													●
2.W.5		●		●			●								●			●		●
2.W.6		●		●			●				●				●			●		●
2.W.7																				
2.W.8												●						●		●
2.L.1		●				●	●		●						●			●		●
2.L.2	●	●				●	●								●			●		●
2.L.3	●	●		●	●	●	●		●	●		●		●	●			●	●	●
2.L.4					●	●							●	●			●			
2.L.5					●															
2.L.6				●											●	●		●		

W = Week

CD-104597 • © Carson-Dellosa

Who Lives at Your House?

Hi, my name is Carla. We have a lot of living things at our house. Some of the living things are people. Some of the living things are animals. We have seven living things at our house.

Day 1

1. The title asks a question. Answer it. _____

   _____

2. Who is telling this story? _____

3. How many living things live at Carla's house? _____

4. What kind of living things are at Carla's house? _____

Four people are in my family. I have a mom, a dad, and a sister named Jamie. We have three pets in our family. We have two cats and one dog.

Day 2

1. How many people live at Carla's house? _____

2. How many animals live at Carla's house? _____

3. Do more **animals** or **people** live there? _____

4. What is Carla's sister's name _____

I live in a house with my family. We live in the country. We have a big backyard. Some people who live near us have horses and cows. We do not have any horses or cows. We have a vegetable garden.

Day 3

1. Where does Carla live: the **city** or the **country**? _____

2. Where do you think she plays: her **backyard** or a **park**? _____

3. List three things you can find in the country. _____

   _____

4. What does Carla **not** have at her house?_____

My cousin lives in the city. He lives in an apartment. He does not have a backyard, animals, or a garden. His neighborhood has a lot of tall buildings. He lives near a park.

Day 4

1. Where does Carla's cousin live: the **city** or the **country**? _____

2. Where do you think he plays: a **backyard** or a **park**? _____

3. List three things you can find in the city.

   _____

4. What does Carla's cousin **not** have at his house?

   _____

Soccer

Carla thinks it is fun to exercise. Her favorite sport is soccer. She plays on a soccer team. Soccer is played on a field shaped like a rectangle. Players move a black-and-white ball to a goal.

You cannot use your hands to hit the ball. You have to kick the ball with your feet. You can also hit the ball with your knee, elbow, or head!

1. What is this passage about?

    _____

2. What is Carla's favorite sport? _____

3. A soccer field is shaped like a . . .

    A.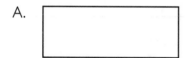

    B.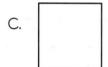

    C.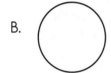

4. When you play soccer, you **cannot** hit the ball with your . . .
    A. head.
    B. elbows.
    C. hands.

5. What is your favorite sport or game? _____

Write the first word of the sentence with a capital letter.

1. (the) _____ flower smells nice.

Circle each picture whose name has a short vowel sound. **Hint:** There may be more than one!

2.

Place a period at the end of the sentence if it tells something or gives a command.

3. Please sit down

Add an **-s** to the noun to make it plural. Write the new word on the line.

4. bird _____

Write the first word of the sentence with a capital letter.

1. (anne) _____ has a black kitten.

Circle each picture whose name has a short vowel sound. **Hint:** There may be more than one!

2.

Place a period at the end of the sentence if it tells something or gives a command.

3. Jose is tired

Add an **-s** to the noun to make it plural. Write the new word on the line.

4. kitten _____

Write the first word of the sentence with a capital letter.

1. (do) _____ you like to play baseball?

Circle each picture whose name has a short vowel sound. **Hint:** There may be more than one!

2.

Place a period at the end of the sentence if it tells something or gives a command.

3. Did you see your sister

Add an **-s** to the noun to make it plural. Write the new word on the line.

4. tree _____

Write the first word of the sentence with a capital letter.

1. (where) _____ is your pen?

Circle each picture whose name has a short vowel sound. **Hint:** There may be more than one!

2.

Place a period at the end of the sentence if it tells something or gives a command.

3. Eat your dinner

Add an **-s** to the noun to make it plural. Write the new word on the line.

4. glove _____

Write the first word of each sentence with a capital letter.

1. (fruit) _____ is a good snack.

2. (turn) _____ on the light.

3. (blue) _____ is my favorite color.

Circle each picture whose name has a short vowel sound.

4.

5.

Place a period at the end of the sentence if it tells something or gives a command.

6. Why is Taylor running

7. That mouse ate all of the cheese

8. My friends sang a song

Add an **-s** to each noun to make it plural. Write the new word on the line.

9. crayon _____

10. egg _____

2.RF.3, 2.L.2, 2.L.3

Day 1

In an instant,
An inchworm inches near.
In an instant,
It can disappear.

1. Read or listen to the poem. Circle each letter **i** that makes the **short i** sound.

2. Write another word or two words for **disappear**. _____

3. About how long is an inchworm?   A. 1 inch   B. 1 foot   C. 1 mile

4. Is an **instant** a long time or a short time? _____

Day 2

Otter likes to play
With many things
Such as olives, octagons,
And big, round rings.

1. Read or listen to the poem. Circle each letter **o** that makes the **short o** sound.

2. What is an **octagon**?   A. number   B. shape   C. car

3. What month's name starts with the **short o** sound? _____

4. Is Otter **serious** or **playful**? _____

Day 3

Oh, I like my overalls,
New or old, striped or bold.
Overalls are great to wear.
I own four pairs, and I won't share!

1. Read or listen to the poem. Circle each letter **o** that makes the **long o** sound.

2. What is the opposite of **new**? _____

3. Line 2 has two opposite words. What are they? _____

4. How many pairs of overalls does the writer own? _____

Day 4

An umbrella goes up.
An umbrella goes down.
People hide under umbrellas
All over town.

1. Read or listen to the poem. Circle each letter **u** that makes the **short u** sound.

2. What is the opposite of **under**? _____

3. This poem has two opposite words. What are they? _____

4. When do you use an umbrella? _____

Weather Puzzle

Use the clues and the words in the word bank to finish the puzzle.

Across

2. Strong wind with rain or snow
3. Drops of water that fall to the earth
5. Loud noise that comes after lightning
6. Moving air

Down

1. Very strong wind that makes a cloud shaped like a funnel
2. Light from the sun
4. Soft, white flakes that fall to the earth

Word Bank

storm   rain   snow

sunshine   wind   thunder

tornado

1. Draw a line to match each word to the type of sound it has.

   soft   long o

   funnel   short i

   snow   short o

   wind   short u

2. Which words in the word bank have a **short u** sound? _____

3. What kind of weather from the word bank is your favorite? _____

4. Which word from the word bank could be called a **funnel cloud**? _____

_____

2.RL.1, 2.RL.10, 2.RI.4, 2.RF.3, 2.L.3, 2.L.4, 2.L.5   CD-104597 • © Carson-Dellosa

Prewrite/Brainstorm

Look at each idea box. Write or draw your ideas in the box.

Pets	School
Toys	Family

Draft

Use your ideas from the idea boxes to finish the sentences.

1. My favorite pet is _____.

2. The toy I like the most is _____.

3. At school, I _____.

4. I live with _____.

Revise

Read the sentences you wrote. Can you make your sentences clearer? Rewrite each sentence.

_____

_____

_____

_____

Proofread

Read the sentences again. Do you see any capitalization errors? Are all of the words spelled correctly? Did you use the correct punctuation and grammar? Use proofreading marks to correct the sentences.

❐ Capitalization mistakes
❐ Grammar mistakes
❐ Punctuation mistakes
❐ Spelling mistakes

Name_____

Publish

Write your final copy on a computer or on the lines below.
MAKE SURE it turns out
- NEAT—Make sure there are no wrinkles, creases, or holes.
- CLEAN—Erase any smudges or dirty spots.
- EASY TO READ—Use your best handwriting and good spacing between words.

_____

_____

_____

_____

_____

_____

_____

_____

_____

_____

_____

_____

Manatees

Manatees are sometimes called sea cows. They are mammals. They must come to the water's surface to breathe air.

1. What does the title say this passage is about? _____

2. What are **manatees**? _____

3. How do manatees get air? _____

4. What is another name for a manatee? _____

West Indian manatees live along the coast of Florida. They are shy and gentle. Manatees are herbivores. This means that they eat only plants. Baby manatees are called calves. They drink their mothers' milk as all mammals do.

1. Which word better describes a manatee: **mean** or **sweet**? _____

2. What is an **herbivore**? _____

3. What are baby manatees called? _____

4. What do manatee calves drink? _____

A habitat is a place where something lives. It is a space that has food, water, air, and shelter. The manatee habitat is changing so fast that manatees are in danger. They are on the endangered animals list.

1. What is a **habitat**? _____

2. What is your habitat? _____

3. What four things does a habitat need? _____

4. Is there a problem with the manatee's habitat? What? _____

_____

Pollutants are harmful things that are sometimes in the water. They can cause manatees to become sick and weak. Manatees must have clean, warm water to live.

1. What are dangerous to manatees? _____

2. What happens to manatees when their water is polluted? _____

3. Who do you think puts pollutants in water: **people** or **plants**? _____

4. What can you do to help keep the water clean for manatees? _____

_____

Warthogs

Warthogs live in Africa. Warthogs got their name from the warts, or bumps, on their faces. They look a lot like pigs.

Warthogs have **tusks**, or long pointed teeth. The tusks stick out from the sides of their mouths. Warthogs use the tusks to **root**, or dig up the ground to look for food. They eat almost anything.

Warthogs also use their tusks to fight. They usually do not choose to fight. They will **flee**, or run away, with their tails sticking up in the air. They hide in **thickets**, or bushes, in the day and come out at night to eat.

1. What does the title say this story is about?

    _____

2. How did warthogs get their name? _____

3. For each sentence, write a word from the paragraph that could take the place of the bold words.

    Warthogs have **pointed teeth**. _____

    Warthogs **dig for food in the ground**. _____

4. For each sentence, write a word from the paragraph that could take the place of the bold words.

    Warthogs live in **bushes**. _____

    Warthogs **run away** from danger. _____

5. Do you think warthogs are beautiful animals? Why or why not? _____

    _____

6. Compare and contrast the habitats of a warthog and a manatee as described on the previous page. _____

    _____

    _____

    _____

2.RI.1, 2.RI.2, 2.RI.4, 2.RI.5, 2.RI.6, 2.RI.9, 2.RI.10, 2.RF.4, 2.W.2, 2.L.4, 2.L.6 CD-104597 • © Carson-Dellosa

Prewrite/Brainstorm

Fill in the character planner about a character from a story or one you have created.

He/she hears:_____

He/she thinks about:_____

He/she says:_____

He/she likes to:_____

He/she feels:_____

He/she goes to:_____

Draft

Write four sentences about the character. Use ideas from your character planner.

_____

_____

_____

_____

Revise

Read the sentences you wrote. Can you make your sentences clearer? Rewrite each sentence.

_____

_____

_____

_____

Proofread

Read the sentences again. Do you see any capitalization errors? Are all of the words spelled correctly? Did you use the correct punctuation and grammar? Use proofreading marks to correct the sentences.

❐ Capitalization mistakes
❐ Grammar mistakes
❐ Punctuation mistakes
❐ Spelling mistakes

Publish

Write your final copy on a computer or on the lines below.

MAKE SURE it turns out

- NEAT—Make sure there are no wrinkles, creases, or holes.
- CLEAN—Erase any smudges or dirty spots.
- EASY TO READ—Use your best handwriting and good spacing between words.

_____

_____

_____

_____

_____

_____

_____

_____

_____

_____

_____

_____

2.RL.3, 2.RI.7, 2.W.5, 2.W.6, 2.L.1, 2.L.2, 2.L.3

Farmer Marcus

Marcus is a farmer. He has an important job. He grows food that we eat. Marcus grows wheat and oats. He also takes care of the animals on his farm. Marcus works hard. He gets up early every day. He works until it is dark.

1. Who is this story about? _____

2. What does he do for a job? _____

3. What does he farm?   plants   animals   both

4. How do you know that Marcus works hard?
   A. He grows wheat and oats.   B. He gets up early and works late.

Day 1

Marcus loves helping the young plants grow. He smiles as he works. In the autumn, he harvests his crops. The wheat is made into bread. The oats are made into cereal.

1. When does Marcus harvest his crops? _____

2. What do you do in the autumn? _____

3. Does the wheat that Marcus grows become **bread** or **lasagna**? _____

4. How do you know that Marcus likes being a farmer?
   A. He smiles as he works.
   B. He harvests his crops.
   C. He grows oats for cereal.

Day 2

Little Miss Muffet sat on her tuffet,
Eating her curds and whey.
Along came a spider and sat down beside her,
And frightened Miss Muffet away.

1. What kind of writing is this: **poem** or **letter**? _____

2. Who is it about? _____

3. Is she eating pasta? _____

4. Circle **True** or **False**. Little Miss Muffet is not afraid of spiders.   **True**   **False**

Day 3

Mary Lou French sat on a bench,
Munching a sandwich and chips.
When Tarantula spied her and climbed up beside her,
She told him to take a long trip!

1. Who is in this poem? _____

2. What is Tarantula: **poisonous spider** or **fuzzy kitten**? _____

3. What is Mary Lou eating? _____

4. Circle **True** or **False**. Mary Lou French is not afraid of spiders.   **True**   **False**

   How do you know? _____

Day 4

Alexander Graham Bell

Alexander Graham Bell did many great things. We know him most for inventing the telephone. But, Alexander had many other talents. He could play music by ear when he was a young boy. He taught music and speech. He also taught the deaf just as his father in Scotland did.

While Alexander was teaching, he became interested in electricity. He and his friend Thomas Watson did many experiments before he invented the telephone.

Alexander stayed busy after inventing the telephone. He created a research laboratory for the deaf. He invented an electric probe used by doctors. He worked on ways to locate icebergs by using echoes. He did many experiments with kites.

1. Have you used a telephone before? _____ Who invented the telephone?

    _____

2. Was Alexander Graham Bell musical? _____

3. Did Alexander give up easily when he was trying to invent the telephone? _____

    Explain your answer. _____

    _____

4. Did Alexander work with the deaf his whole life or only when he was young? _____

    _____

5. Find and circle the six words in the box that best describe Alexander.

afraid	funny	smart
busy	hard-working	strong
clumsy	mean	talented
creative	musical	uncaring

2.RL.1, 2.RL.3, 2.RL.4, 2.RI.1, 2.RI.10, 2.RF.4, 2.L.1, 2.L.6

Name_____

Circle the letters that should be capitalized.

1. the science report is due monday.

Underline the verb in the sentence.

2. She hides under the bed.

Create your own question. Remember to add a question mark at the end of the sentence.

3. Who _____

If a noun ends in **s**, **ss**, **sh**, **ch**, or **x**, add **-es** to make it plural. Underline the letter or letters at the end of the word that tell you how to make the plural. Write the new word on the line.

4. glass _____

Circle the letters that should be capitalized.

1. tom's birthday is november 4.

Underline the verb in the sentence.

2. We eat pizza for lunch.

Create your own question. Remember to add a question mark at the end of the sentence.

3. What _____

If a noun ends in **s**, **ss**, **sh**, **ch**, or **x**, add **-es** to make it plural. Underline the letter or letters at the end of the word that tell you how to make the plural. Write the new word on the line.

4. match _____

Circle the letters that should be capitalized.
1. see dr. patel on wednesday.

Underline the verb in the sentence.

2. I swim on a team.

Create your own question. Remember to add a question mark at the end of the sentence.

3. When _____

If a noun ends in **s**, **ss**, **sh**, **ch**, or **x**, add **-es** to make it plural. Underline the letter or letters at the end of the word that tell you how to make the plural. Write the new word on the line.

4. gas _____

Circle the letters that should be capitalized.

1. soccer practice is on thursday.

Underline the verb in the sentence.

2. The bunny hops.

Create your own question. Remember to add a question mark at the end of the sentence.

3. Where _____

If a noun ends in **s**, **ss**, **sh**, **ch**, or **x**, add **-es** to make it plural. Underline the letter or letters at the end of the word that tell you how to make the plural. Write the new word on the line.

4. watch _____

Circle the letters that should be capitalized.

1. our pizza party is on saturday.

2. we always make crafts in november and december.

Underline the verb in the sentence.

3. Grace dances at school.

4. You laugh at everything!

5. Throw your trash in the bin.

Create your own questions. Remember to add a question mark at the end of each sentence.

6. Why _____

7. How _____

If a noun ends in **s**, **ss**, **sh**, **ch**, or **x**, add **-es** to make it plural. Underline the letter or letters at the end of each word that tell you how to make the plural. Write the new word on the line.

8. tax _____

9. brush _____

10. switch _____

Barker's Big Problem

Barker wished she was the biggest dog on the block. Every time Barker saw Bruiser, she hung her head. "I'll never be that big," she thought. "What good is a little dog? A big dog can carry newspapers. She can chase away pesky cats."

1. Which word is a compound word? A. wished B. biggest C. newspapers

2. Which word could you use instead of **pesky**? A. annoying B. darling

3. Is Barker **happy** or **jealous**? _____

4. What does Barker wish for? _____

Day 1

One day, Barker jogged along the sidewalk. "Help!" someone cried. Barker ran to check out the problem. Bruiser stood nearby.

1. Circle the compound words.
   sidewalk   problem   someone   nearby

2. What other word could you use instead of **jogged**? _____

3. Barker runs to the sound of someone crying for help. What does that tell you about Barker's character? _____

4. Whom does Barker see at the scene of the problem? _____

Day 2

"A boy is caught in the bushes on the other side of the wall," Bruiser said. "There's a small hole, but I can't wriggle through."

1. Do you pronounce the **w** at the beginning of **wriggled**? _____

2. What does it mean that the boy is caught in the bushes: has **he grabbed the bushes** or have **the bushes grabbed him**? _____

   _____

3. What is Bruiser's problem? _____

4. What do you think happens next? _____

Day 3

Barker trotted through the hole. She tugged on the branches wrapped around the boy's ankle. She got him free. "Thank you!" said the boy. The boy hugged Barker and patted her head.

1. Do you pronounce the **w** at the beginning of **wrapped**? _____

2. Which word could you use instead of **tugged**: **snipped** or **pulled**? _____

3. What is the main idea of this story?
   A. Barker learned only little dogs can help people.
   B. Barker learned both big and little dogs can help people.

4. How do you think Barker feels about her size now? _____

Day 4

Jackie Joyner-Kersee

Who is Jackie Joyner-Kersee? Is she a wrestler? Is she a writer? No! She is a world-class track star. Jackie Joyner-Kersee loves to compete in track events. She runs, jumps hurdles, throws a shot put (a metal ball), and throws the javelin (a long spear). She won many Olympic medals. She is a great athlete.

Jackie has asthma. This is an illness that makes it hard for her to breathe. When a person has asthma, it is hard to take a breath and get air in the lungs. Coughing and wheezing are also parts of asthma. Asthma makes it hard for Jackie to run and jump. Jackie did not let asthma stop her from competing and winning races. She worked hard. She is known as the greatest multi-event athlete in women's track history!

1. Circle each word that has a **w** you do not pronounce.

    wrestler   world   wheezing   writer

2. What is a **javelin**? _____

3. What is the main idea of this passage?
    A. Some athletes have asthma.
    B. Track athletes work hard.
    C. Jackie Joyner-Kersee did not let asthma stop her from competing and being the best.

4. Underline the two sentences in the passage that tell you why having asthma makes it hard to be a track athlete.

5. What does the passage tell us about Jackie's character: that she is **determined** or that she is **lazy**? _____

2.RL.1, 2.RL.4, 2.RI.1, 2.RI.4, 2.RI.6, 2.RI.10, 2.RF.3, 2.RF.4, 2.L.2, 2.L.4

Prewrite/Brainstorm

Think of words that rhyme with **dot**. Write them in the word web.

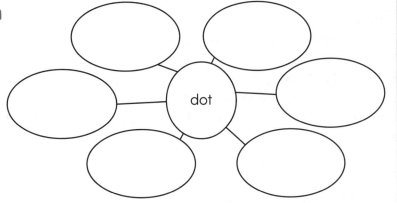

Draft

Write four silly sentences that rhyme. Use words from your rhyming word web.

_____

_____

_____

_____

Revise

Read the sentences you wrote. Can you make your sentences clearer? Rewrite each sentence.

_____

_____

_____

_____

Proofread

Read the sentences again. Do you see any capitalization errors? Are all of the words spelled correctly? Did you use the correct punctuation and grammar? Use proofreading marks to correct the sentences.

❏ Capitalization mistakes
❏ Grammar mistakes
❏ Punctuation mistakes
❏ Spelling mistakes

Publish

Write your final copy on a computer or on the lines below.
MAKE SURE it turns out
- NEAT—Make sure there are no wrinkles, creases, or holes.
- CLEAN—Erase any smudges or dirty spots.
- EASY TO READ—Use your best handwriting and good spacing between words.

_____

_____

_____

_____

_____

_____

_____

_____

_____

_____

_____

_____

The clock showed midnight. Two mice sat in their home. They talked about the things they wanted to do. One wanted to eat all of the cheese in the world. The other wanted to break all of the mousetraps in the world.

1. Where does this story happen? _____

2. When does this story happen? _____

3. What do you call more than one mouse? _____

4. Do you think the mice can really do what they are talking about? _____

   Why or why not? _____

Juan and Dylan went to school early in the morning. They sat at their desks. The teacher read a book about dolphins. Then, Juan and Dylan wrote books of their own.

1. Where does this story happen? _____

2. When does this story happen? _____

3. Who are the people in this story? _____

4. Do you write books at school? _____

   What do you write about? _____

The year is 3010. Renee and Rashad zoom into space. Their spaceship moves faster than the speed of light. They race toward the moon.

1. Where does this story happen? _____

2. When does this story happen? _____

3. Where are Renee and Rashad going? _____

4. Would you like to go to the moon? _____

   Why or why not? _____

Chester was hungry. He ran down the tree trunk. He pawed at the dead leaves. He wanted the nut he had hidden yesterday. He dug and dug. It was not there! He looked at all of the other trees. Now, where did he hide that nut?

1. Where does this story happen? _____

2. When does this story happen? _____

3. What is Chester?   dog   blue jay   squirrel

4. What did Chester lose? _____

A Special Place

Maggie is at Grandma's house. She loves the kitchen.

Pretty curtains with dots hang on the windows. The walls are bright yellow. There is a table with six chairs. Many cupboards hold dishes, pots and pans, and food.

Grandma has magnets in her kitchen. They are so colorful. Maggie loves to look at them. She also loves to watch Grandma bake. Grandma makes many good things. Right now, Grandma is frosting a cake.

1. Where did this story take place?

    _____

2. What is the special place? _____

    _____

3. What is pretty about the kitchen? _____

4. What two things does Maggie love to see in the kitchen? _____

    _____

5. Describe a place that is special to you. (Example: I love my basement stairs because they are dark and have a lot of spiderwebs.)

    _____

    _____

    _____

    _____

2.RL.1, 2.RL.9, 2.RF.4, 2.W.1, 2.W.8, 2.L.6

Prewrite/Brainstorm

How are turtles and fish alike? How are they different? Fill in the Venn diagram.

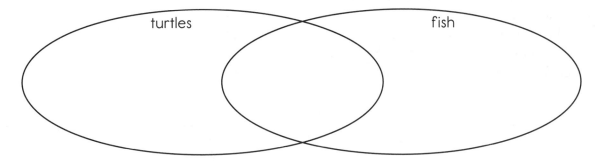

turtles   fish

Draft

Write a few sentences that tell how turtles and fish are alike and different. Use your ideas from the diagram. Would you like a turtle or a fish for a pet? Why?

_____

_____

_____

_____

Revise

Read the sentences you wrote. Can you make your sentences clearer? Rewrite each sentence.

_____

_____

_____

_____

Proofread

Read the sentences again. Do you see any capitalization errors? Are all of the words spelled correctly? Did you use the correct punctuation and grammar? Use proofreading marks to correct the sentences.

❏ Capitalization mistakes
❏ Grammar mistakes
❏ Punctuation mistakes
❏ Spelling mistakes

Publish

Write your final copy on a computer or on the lines below.
MAKE SURE it turns out
- NEAT—Make sure there are no wrinkles, creases, or holes.
- CLEAN—Erase any smudges or dirty spots.
- EASY TO READ—Use your best handwriting and good spacing between words.

_____

_____

_____

_____

_____

_____

_____

_____

_____

_____

_____

_____

_____

"Good morning, Mom," said Lamar, as he raced down the stairs. "What time do we leave for vacation? I can hardly wait!"

1. What time of day does this story take place? _____

2. Where does this story take place? _____

3. Predict what is about to happen. _____

_____

4. Does the story tell you if it is winter or summer? _____

Day 1

"The lake is the best!" said Ana. She leaned against a tree. "I really like it when the sun starts to go down. I'm ready to tell scary stories."

1. What time of day does this story take place? _____

2. Where does this story take place? _____

3. Predict what is about to happen. _____

_____

4. Does the story tell you if Ana is staying in a tent or a cabin? _____

Day 2

The submarine moved deep in the ocean. Eric saw fish and an octopus outside the window. He looked at his watch. "It's so dark down here. It does not seem like four o'clock," he thought.

1. What time of day does this story take place? _____

2. When is that time of day?   A. the afternoon   B. the middle of the night

3. Where does this story take place? _____

4. What does Eric see in this setting that he cannot see at home? _____

_____

Day 3

"Brrrr! It's so cold here on top of the mountain in the middle of the night." Sasha pulled her hat over her ears. Soon, it would be time to go back down the mountain.

1. What time of day does this story take place? _____

2. Where does this story take place? _____

3. Predict what is about to happen. _____

4. What other detail do we learn about the mountain? _____

_____

Day 4

All in a Day's Work

Zookeepers care for the animals in zoos every day. They make the animals' food and keep the animal homes clean. They spend a lot of time watching the animals to make sure they are healthy.

Zookeepers also have to keep the animals from getting bored. In the wild, the animals' habitats are always changing. At the zoo, the animals' homes stay the same. A good zookeeper will think of ways for the animals to have fun.

One way to keep the animals happy is to hide their food. The animals enjoy looking for their food because it is a little bit like hunting. To keep animals curious, zookeepers also put safe plants from other places or different smells in the animal homes.

1. Was this story about a vacation? _____

    Why or why not? _____

2. Where does this story take place? _____

3. What is different about the zoo for the animals?
    A. They are around other animals.
    B. The settings stay the same.
    C. The food is better.

4. What do zookeepers do to help the animals feel like they are hunting?

    _____

5. Would you like to be a zookeeper? _____ Why or why not?

    _____

    _____

    _____

Circle the letters that should be capitalized.

1.

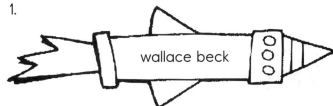

Write **C** next to each common noun and **P** next to each proper noun.

2. April _____ dog _____

Put the correct ending mark (**.** **?** **!**) at the end of the sentence.

3. That bunny is so cute

Underline the word that is incorrect. Add a silent **-e** to the word and write it on the line.

4. Sally at the crunchy apple.

_____

Circle the letters that should be capitalized.

1.

Write **C** next to each common noun and **P** next to each proper noun.

2. Wednesday _____ Fifi _____

Put the correct ending mark (**.** **?** **!**) at the end of the sentence.

3. Do you have a pet

Underline the word that is incorrect. Add a silent **-e** to the word and write it on the line.

4. The clown gave Tom a candy can.

_____

Circle the letters that should be capitalized.

1.

Write **C** next to each common noun and **P** next to each proper noun.

2. Pacific _____ lake _____

Put the correct ending mark (**.** **?** **!**) at the end of the sentence.

3. My cat loves tuna

Underline the word that is incorrect. Add a silent **-e** to the word and write it on the line.

4. I want to fly my kit.

_____

Circle the letters that should be capitalized.

1.

Write **C** next to each common noun and **P** next to each proper noun.

2. boy _____ Italy _____

Put the correct ending mark (**.** **?** **!**) at the end of the sentence.

3. I think turtles are fun

Underline the word that is incorrect. Add a silent **-e** to the word and write it on the line.

4. Jared took car of his puppy.

_____

Name_____

Circle the letters that should be capitalized.

1.

uncle frederico

2.

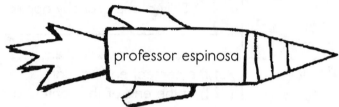
professor espinosa

3.

miss julia freeman

Write **C** next to each common noun and **P** next to each proper noun.

4.   Raul _____

5.   flower _____

6.   country_____

Place the correct ending mark (**. ? !**) at the end of each sentence.

7.   Look at that

8.   Have you ever seen a ferret

Underline the word that is incorrect. Add a silent **-e** to the word and write it on the line.

9.   Rip peaches are good to eat. _____

10.   Mom wrote a not to my teacher. _____

The Loose Tooth Diaries

I have a loose tooth. This is my very first loose tooth! Today, I spent a lot of time wiggling my very first loose tooth. I cannot wait for it to come out!

1. Does the **oo** in **loose** have the same sound as the **oo** in **tooth**? _____

2. How do you wiggle a tooth: **move it back and forth** or **blow on it**?

    _____

3. How much time did Trisha spend wiggling her tooth? _____

4. Circle **True** or **False**. Trisha is scared to lose her tooth.   **True   False**

    Underline the sentence that helped you figure this out.

Day 1

I can wiggle my tooth with my tongue. It is getting really loose! Today, I tried to eat an apple. My loose tooth made it impossible! It really hurt. My mom cut the apple into pieces for me.

1. Which word rhymes with **tongue**: **song** or **sung**? _____

2. What does **impossible** mean? _____

3. What is this paragraph mostly about: **Trisha's tooth has come out** or **Trisha's tooth is getting really loose**? _____

4. Underline one sentence that helped you answer question 3.

Day 2

Today, I took a bite of my sandwich, and my tooth popped out! It hurt a little bit. I went into the bathroom. I rinsed my mouth with water. When I touch the space with my tongue, it feels funny! Tonight, I will put my tooth under my pillow. I cannot wait!

1. Find one other word that has the same **i** sound as **bite**. Write it. _____

2. When you rinse your mouth, do you **drink the water** or **spit it out**?

    _____

3. What is this paragraph mostly about: **how Trisha's tooth came out** or **how to eat a sandwich**? _____

4. Underline one sentence that helped you answer question 3.

Day 3

I woke up this morning and found a note under my pillow. It was from the tooth fairy! It said my tooth is nice and shiny. She also left me some money. I could get rich if I lose all of my teeth!

1. Does the **i** in **shiny** sound the same as the **i** in **nice** or the **i** in **rich**? _____

2. What other word could you use instead of **shiny**? _____

3. What is this paragraph mostly about: **what the tooth fairy leaves every child** or **what the tooth fairy left for Trisha**? _____

4. Do you think Trisha will get rich if she loses all of her teeth? _____

    Why or why not? _____

Day 4

Who Comes for the Teeth?

Many children around the world believe that a mouse comes to take their teeth when they lose them.

In South Africa, children place their teeth in slippers. They believe that a mouse comes into their rooms when they are sleeping. The mouse takes each tooth and leaves a small gift.

In Venezuela, children leave their teeth under their pillows. They believe that a mouse called El Ratón Pérez takes the teeth and leaves money.

In Spain, children also place their teeth under their pillows. They believe that a mouse named Ratoncita Pérez takes the teeth and leaves money or candy.

In Russia, mothers place the teeth into mouse holes.

Many customs around the world include a mouse instead of a tooth fairy. Do you think a mouse comes for your teeth too?

1.   Circle each word where the letter in bold sounds the same as the **i** in **into**.

   g**i**ft   th**i**nk   m**i**ce   sl**i**pper

2.   What word from the story means "more than one mouse"? _____

3.   What is the main idea of the story?
   A.   Many children believe that a mouse comes for their teeth.
   B.   Some children place their teeth in slippers.
   C.   Some mothers place teeth into mouse holes.

4.   Which countries' people believe that a mouse will bring money for lost teeth?

   _____

5.   Circle **True** or **False**. There is only one country where kids get presents for lost teeth.

   True   **False**

Prewrite/Brainstorm

Choose a topic. Fill in the chart with facts and your opinions about the topic.

Topic	
Facts	Opinions

Day 1

Draft

Write a paragraph about your topic. Use two facts and one opinion from the chart.

_____

_____

_____

_____

Day 2

Revise

Read the sentences you wrote. Can you make your sentences clearer? Rewrite each sentence. Be sure to use specific nouns and verbs.

_____

_____

_____

_____

Day 3

Proofread

Read the sentences again. Do you see any capitalization errors? Are all of the words spelled correctly? Did you use the correct punctuation and grammar? Use proofreading marks to correct the sentences.

- ❑ Capitalization mistakes
- ❑ Grammar mistakes
- ❑ Punctuation mistakes
- ❑ Spelling mistakes

Day 4

Publish

Write your final copy on a computer or on the lines below.
MAKE SURE it turns out

- NEAT—Make sure there are no wrinkles, creases, or holes.
- CLEAN—Erase any smudges or dirty spots.
- EASY TO READ—Use your best handwriting and good spacing between words.

_____

_____

_____

_____

_____

_____

_____

_____

_____

_____

_____

_____

Name_____

Animals on the Move

Many animals migrate. They move from one place to another. Some move because they cannot find food. Others move to find a better place to raise their young.

Day 1

1. What does **migrate** mean?   A. move from one place to another   B. stay put

2. Does the paragraph talk about a specific animal? _____

3. Place an **X** next to the main idea of this paragraph.
    _____ Some animals move because it is cold where they live.
    _____ Many animals migrate.

4. Write one detail that supports the main idea. _____

Many birds migrate south in the winter. They cannot find enough food where it is cold. They fly south where it is warm. There, they find food for the winter. When winter is over, they fly north.

Day 2

1. Do all birds migrate south in the winter? _____

2. Fill in the blank. Warm weather = a lot of food. Cold weather = _____

3. Place an **X** next to the main idea of this paragraph.
    _____ Birds migrate south so that they can find food.
    _____ When winter is over, birds fly north.

4. Write one detail that supports the main idea. _____

Some whales spend summers in the cold waters of the Arctic. When it begins to freeze, the whales swim to warmer seas. They have their babies in warm water because the babies do not have a thick layer of blubber to keep them warm.

Day 3

1. Do all whales live in the Arctic? _____

2. When do whales have babies: **winter** or **summer**? _____

3. Place an **X** next to the main idea of this paragraph.
    _____ Some whales migrate to warm waters to have their babies.
    _____ Baby whales do not have blubber.

4. Write one detail that supports the main idea. _____

Salmon are fish that are usually born in freshwater streams. They migrate to the ocean where they eat shrimp, squid, and small fish. When salmon are ready to lay eggs, they return to the streams where they were born.

Day 4

1. What do salmon eat? _____

2. Do salmon lay eggs in the **ocean** or in their **home streams**? _____

3. Place an **X** next to the main idea of this paragraph.
    _____ Salmon migrate from freshwater streams to the ocean.
    _____ Salmon eat shrimp, squid, and small fish.

4. Write one detail that supports the main idea. _____

Muscles Are Movers

Your body has more than 600 muscles. Exercise makes muscles bigger and stronger. Your muscles are at work all day long. They lift, push, and pull. Muscles work at night too.

Some muscles are called voluntary muscles. They move when you want them to move. Most movements use voluntary muscles. Raising your hand and stretching your legs to run are examples. The brain controls voluntary muscles.

Other muscles move or work for you. These are called involuntary muscles. Involuntary muscles work without you thinking about them. They work all of the time. Your heart pumps blood, and your intestines help digest food. These are examples of involuntary muscles.

1. What is the main idea of this passage?

   _____

   _____

   _____

2. The main idea of the first paragraph is: **Your muscles are at work.** Write two details from the first paragraph that support the main idea.

   _____

   _____

3. The main idea of the second paragraph is: **Voluntary muscles move when you want them to move.** Write two details from the second paragraph that support the main idea.

   _____

   _____

4. Underline the sentence that is the main idea of the last paragraph.

5. Imagine that you just yawned. Is that an example of a voluntary or involuntary use of your muscles? _____

Name_____

Prewrite/Brainstorm

Sometimes, you write about a chain of events. Think about a chain of events. Fill in the chart. List the events in the order that they happen. If you need more room, write them on another sheet of paper.

Topic
First,
Next,
Then,
Next,
Then,
Finally,

Day 1

Draft

Read your list of events. Write a paragraph that contains all of the events.

_____

_____

_____

_____

Day 2

Revise

Read the paragraph you wrote. Did you write the events in the order that they happened? Can you make your sentences clearer? Rewrite the paragraph. Be sure to use specific nouns and verbs.

_____

_____

_____

_____

Day 3

Proofread

Read the paragraph again. Do you see any capitalization errors? Are all of the words spelled correctly? Did you use the correct punctuation and grammar? Use proofreading marks to correct the sentences.

- ❐ Capitalization mistakes
- ❐ Grammar mistakes
- ❐ Punctuation mistakes
- ❐ Spelling mistakes

Day 4

Publish

Write your final copy on a computer or on the lines below.
MAKE SURE it turns out
- NEAT—Make sure there are no wrinkles, creases, or holes.
- CLEAN—Erase any smudges or dirty spots.
- EASY TO READ—Use your best handwriting and good spacing between words.

_____

_____

_____

_____

_____

_____

_____

_____

_____

_____

_____

_____

2.RL.5, 2.RI.3, 2.RI.7, 2.W.5, 2.W.6, 2.L.1, 2.L.2, 2.L.3

Scary Sleepover

"Did you hear that noise?" asked Ellen.

"What was it?" asked Ava.

The girls pulled their sleeping bags up to their chins. Their hands shook with fright as they listened in the darkness.

1. Who is in this story? _____

2. What time of day is it?   A. 10 o'clock in the morning   B. 10 o'clock at night

3. How do the girls feel? _____

4. What makes them feel that way? _____

"There it is again. Do you think it's the troll from the scary story you told?" asked Ellen.

A light flashed outside the tent. The girls heard footsteps coming slowly toward them. The tent zipper slowly began to rise. The girls let out screams that could be heard for miles.

1. What did the girls do that night?   A. tell scary stories   B. read nursery rhymes

2. Where are the girls? _____

3. What do they do when the zipper goes up? _____

4. What would you do? _____

"What's all the noise?" asked Ava's mother. "Are you two all right?" She poked her head inside the tent. She moved her flashlight inside to see what was frightening the girls.

1. What scared the girls: **a troll** or **Ava's mother**? _____

2. What is the setting of this story?
   A. Ava's bedroom   B. Ava's backyard   C. Ellen's backyard

3. How does Ava's mother feel: **worried about the girls** or **worried about her grass**? _____

4. Do you think Ava and Ellen were happy to see Ava's mother? _____

Ava and Ellen sighed. "We told too many scary stories," said Ava. "I think we want to sleep in the house tonight after all! Camping in the backyard isn't as fun as we thought it would be."

1. Predict what will happen next. _____

   _____

2. What would you have done if you were Ava or Ellen? _____

3. Why did the author write this story?
   A. to tell you about a camping trip   B. to keep you from going camping

4. Would you like to go camping in a backyard? _____

The Grasshopper and the Ant

A grasshopper was singing on a hot summer day. He watched a little ant drag a heavy piece of corn through the grass.

"Come play with me," the grasshopper called out. "It is much too pretty a day to work so hard."

"I do not have time to play," said the ant. "Winter is coming. It will be hard to find food then, so I am storing food now. Then, I will have plenty to eat when snow is on the ground."

The grasshopper laughed. "Why worry about winter now? It is so far away. A lot of food is here to eat today."

The ant just smiled and walked on.

When winter came, the grasshopper showed up at the ant's door.

"I am very hungry. Could you please give me some food?" the grasshopper asked.

"I only have enough for me," said the ant. "You should have planned ahead."

1. Name the characters in this story.

   _____

2. When does this story take place? _____

3. What sentence could be added to the beginning of the fifth paragraph above?
   A. Grasshoppers have long back legs they use for jumping.
   B. "You should store food for the winter too," said the ant.
   C. Ants keep their food in special rooms in their underground homes.

4. What did the ant mean when he said, "You should have planned ahead"?

   _____

5. Why did the author write this story?
   A. to make you feel sad for the grasshopper
   B. to tell how ants store food for winter
   C. to teach an important lesson

Read the song title. Rewrite the title with the correct capital letters.

1. "Mary had a little lamb" _____

Read the sentence. Circle the helping verb. Underline the main verb.

2. Next week, I will sing in the school talent show.

Read the sentence. Add commas if they are needed.

3. My mother grows roses daisies and violets in her garden.

Write **Your** or **You're** to correctly complete the sentence.

4. _____ invited to my sleepover.

Day 1

Read the book title. Rewrite the title with the correct capital letters.

1. *the biography of helen keller* _____

Read the sentence. Circle the helping verb. Underline the main verb.

2. Someday, I will teach my dog to fetch.

Read the sentence. Add commas if they are needed.

3. My brother's name is John Henry Mills.

Write **your** or **you're** to correctly complete the sentence.

4. Please bring _____ sleeping bag.

Day 2

Read the magazine title. Rewrite the title with the correct capital letters.

1. *horse lover magazine* _____

Read the sentence. Circle the helping verb. Underline the main verb.

2. After school, Carter can come to my house to play.

Read the sentence. Add commas if they are needed.

3. My street has maple pine oak and elm trees.

Write **Your** or **You're** to correctly complete the sentence.

4. _____ welcome to bring your dog.

Day 3

Read the book title. Rewrite the title with the correct capital letters.

1. *green eggs and ham* _____

Read the sentence. Circle the helping verb. Underline the main verb.

2. Jeff can watch the movie with me tonight.

Read the sentence. Add commas if they are needed.

3. We study spelling math history and art.

Write **Your** or **You're** to correctly complete the sentence.

4. _____ mom will drive you to my house.

Day 4

Read the titles. Rewrite the titles with the correct capital letters.

1. "twinkle, twinkle, little star" _____

2. *the big book of lizards* _____

Read the sentences. Circle the helping verbs. Underline the main verbs.

3. Amy will write her report after class.

4. The bird can fly, now that her wing is healed.

5. The sun will rise tomorrow.

Read the sentences. Add commas if they are needed.

6. Claire Phil Taneshia Joey and I went to the movies together.

7. Tara brought a blanket food drinks and games to the park.

8. Mona's favorite colors are yellow purple blue and pink.

Write **your** or **you're** to correctly complete the sentences.

9. You have to call _____ parents.

10. I think _____ going to love my new game!

2.L.1, 2.L.2, 2.L.3

Cat Problems

Each day, the cat chased the mice. The mice had to hide. They could not hunt for food. They were hungry.

1. When you say **each**, how many sounds does **ea** have?
A. one (as in **ear**)   B. two

2. Which word could you use instead of **hungry**?
A. full   B. starving

3. Who are the characters in the story? _____

4. Why are the mice unable to hunt for food? _____

"What can we do?" said Mother Mouse. "I don't know," said the biggest mouse. "I don't know," said the oldest mouse. "I don't know," said the tallest mouse.

1. Which word in this paragraph rhymes with **show** and has a silent letter? _____

2. What does **don't** mean: **donut** or **do not**? _____

3. How many mice are in the story so far? _____

4. Do the mice think of a solution to their problem? _____

"I know," said the smallest mouse. "Let's hang a bell around the cat's neck. Then, when we hear him coming, we can run."
Everyone cheered. They told the smallest mouse how smart she was.

1. Does the **k** in **know** have a sound, or is it a silent letter? _____

2. What does **let's** mean: **let us** or **lettuce**? _____

3. Who thinks of a solution to the problem? _____

4. What is the solution? _____
_____

Then, the oldest mouse said, "That is a good idea, but we still have a problem. Who will put the bell on the cat?"

1. When you say **idea**, how many sounds does the **ea** have?
A. one (as in **pea**)   B. two

2. Are any mice older than the **oldest mouse**? _____

3. Was the smallest mouse's idea a good solution to the problem? _____

4. What new problem does the solution cause? _____
_____

Who Is Lost?

Maria looked into her pet's cage. Henry should have been asleep in his nest. But, he was not there! Then, Maria saw the open cage door. Where did Henry go?

Maria looked all around the cage. She looked on the floor. She looked under her bed. She did not find him. She did not know what to do.

Maria felt like crying as she got dressed for school. She sat to put on her shoes. First, she put on the left shoe. Then, she picked up the right shoe. It felt heavy. Guess who she found in her shoe?

1. Circle the words from the story that rhyme with **show**.

    shoe   go   no   know   who

    Which word has a silent letter? _____

2. Circle three words you could use when something was there and then it was gone.

    vanished   disappeared   underneath   missing

3. Who are the characters in the story? _____

4. What is Maria's problem? _____

5. How is her problem solved? _____

    _____

    _____

    _____

2.RL.1, 2.RL.3, 2.RF.3, 2.L.2, 2.L.3

Name_____

Prewrite/Brainstorm

Lamar likes ice cream. His teacher wants to know why he likes it. Help Lamar by filling out the idea sundae.

I Like Ice Cream

Draft

Write a paragraph about why Lamar likes ice cream. Use the ideas from your idea sundae.

_____

_____

_____

_____

Revise

Read the paragraph you wrote. Did you use all of your ideas? Can you make your sentences clearer? Rewrite the paragraph. Be sure to use specific nouns and verbs.

_____

_____

_____

_____

Proofread

Read your paragraph again. Do you see any capitalization errors? Are all of the words spelled correctly? Did you use the correct punctuation and grammar? Use proofreading marks to correct the sentences.

- ❒ Capitalization mistakes
- ❒ Grammar mistakes
- ❒ Punctuation mistakes
- ❒ Spelling mistakes

Publish

Write your final copy on a computer or on the lines below.
MAKE SURE it turns out

- NEAT—Make sure there are no wrinkles, creases, or holes.
- CLEAN—Erase any smudges or dirty spots.
- EASY TO READ—Use your best handwriting and good spacing between words.

_____

_____

_____

_____

_____

_____

_____

_____

_____

_____

_____

_____

Baby Animal Names

Many animals are called special names when they are young. A baby deer is called a fawn. A baby cat is called a kitten.

1. What is the name of a baby deer? _____

2. What is the name of a baby cat? _____

3. What is the name of a young person? _____

4. Have you ever seen a fawn or a kitten? _____

   Describe it. _____

Day 1

Some baby animals have the same names as other kinds of baby animals. A baby elephant is a calf. A baby whale is a calf. A baby giraffe is a calf. A baby cow is a calf.

1. How many baby animals are called calves? _____

2. Name each baby animal that is called a calf. _____

   _____

3. Which calves are wild animals? _____

4. Which calves live on a farm? _____

Day 2

Some baby animals are called cubs. A baby lion, a baby bear, a baby tiger, and a baby fox are all called cubs.

1. How many baby animals are called cubs? _____

2. Name the baby animals that are called cubs. _____

   _____

3. Which cubs are wild animals? _____

4. Which cubs are big cats? _____

Day 3

Some baby animals are called colts. A baby horse is a colt. A baby zebra is a colt. A baby donkey is a colt.

1. How many baby animals are called colts? _____

2. Name the baby animals that are called colts. _____

3. Which colts are wild animals? _____

4. Use your answers above to help you fill in the chart. Write one animal that belongs with each baby name.

calf	cub	colt

Day 4

What Is in My Room?

Sometimes, you want to put things in groups. One way to put things in groups is to sort them by how they are alike. When you put things together that are alike in some way, you classify them.

You can classify the things in your room. In one group, you can put toys and fun things. In the other group, you can put things that you wear.

1. What is the setting of this passage?

    _____

2. Circle the words that also mean **classify**.

    group   sort   things

3. Circle all of the things you can wear.

    hat   doll   shirt
    truck   mitten   shoe
    ball   paints   shorts
    sock   book   teddy bear

4. Fill in the chart using the words above.

Things I Play With	Things I Wear

5. Add something to each category that you have in your room.

2.RL.4, 2.RI.1, 2.RI.10, 2.RF.4

Name_____

Prewrite/Brainstorm

Look at the picture.
What are the kids doing?
Fill in the chart with the
five W's about the picture.

Who?	What?	When?	Where?	Why?

Draft

Write a paragraph about the picture. Use the five W's from the chart.

_____

_____

_____

_____

Revise

Read the paragraph you wrote. Did you include all five W's? Are the words in the right order? Are your word groups sentences? Rewrite your paragraph.

_____

_____

_____

_____

Proofread

Read your paragraph again. Do you see any capitalization errors? Are all of the words spelled correctly? Did you use the correct punctuation and grammar? Use proofreading marks to correct the sentences.

- ❏ Capitalization mistakes
- ❏ Grammar mistakes
- ❏ Punctuation mistakes
- ❏ Spelling mistakes

Publish

Write your final copy on a computer or on the lines below.
MAKE SURE it turns out

- NEAT—Make sure there are no wrinkles, creases, or holes.
- CLEAN—Erase any smudges or dirty spots.
- EASY TO READ—Use your best handwriting and good spacing between words.

_____

_____

_____

_____

_____

_____

_____

_____

_____

_____

_____

Lisa's Game

Lisa hurried. She did not want to be late for her softball game. All of a sudden, wings grew on her back. She flew all the way to the field.

1. Write the words from the story that rhyme with **new**. _____
   Circle each word that has one syllable.

2. Which word could you use instead of **all of a sudden**?
   A. quickly   B. suddenly

3. Could this story really happen? _____

4. Underline the sentences that are not possible in the real world.

Day 1

Alex's Garden

The hot summer sun dried out the garden. Alex wanted his flowers to grow. He got the hose and watered his flowers.

1. Does the **ow** in **flowers** sound the same as the **ow** in **grow**? _____

2. What is the opposite of a **growing plant**?
   A. dead plant   B. short plant

3. Could this story really happen? _____

4. Underline the sentences that are not possible in the real world.

Day 2

Keenan's Present

Keenan saved money all month. He wanted to buy a special gift for his grandfather. He bought a book about stereos. He knew his grandfather would love it.

1. Write the words that have three syllables. _____

   Which word starts with **st**? _____

2. Cross out the word **gift**. Write another word for **gift**. _____

3. Could this story really happen? _____

4. Underline the sentences that are not possible in the real world.

Day 3

Michelle's Stairs

Michelle learned about the stars. She learned about the planet Mars. Michelle pulled stars from the sky. She made stairs from the stars. She walked all the way up her starry staircase to Mars.

1. Write all of the words that start with **st**. _____

   Which words have two syllables? _____

2. Cross out **walked**. Write another way to go up a staircase. _____

3. Could this story really happen? _____

4. Underline the sentences that are not possible in the real world.

Day 4

Talk to the Animals

Can a gorilla talk? Gorillas do not form words the way humans do. But, they can make known what they want to say. One gorilla, Koko, learned sign language. She talked with her hands. And, she understood words humans said.

Dr. Penny Patterson is the scientist who taught sign language to Koko. She showed Koko a picture of the two of them together. Penny pointed to Koko in the picture and asked, "Who's that?"

Koko answered by signing her own name, Koko.

1. Write the words from this passage that have three syllables. _____

   _____

   Which word has **st** in the middle? _____

2. What is another word for **humans**? _____

3. What is it called when you talk with your hands? _____

4. What is the name of the gorilla in this passage? _____

5. Do you think this story really happened? _____

   Why or why not? _____

   _____

   _____

   _____

 2.RI.1, 2.RI.4, 2.RI.10, 2.RF.3, 2.RF.4, 2.L.3, 2.L.5 CD-104597 • © Carson-Dellosa

Day 1

Circle the letters that should be capitalized.
1.   my friends and i go to bear creek school.
If the group of words is a complete sentence, color the fish purple. If the group of words is not a sentence, color the fish green.
2.   Fish eat worms.
Add quotation marks around what the person said.
3.   Jill won a medal, yelled the coach.
Some words sound alike but have different meanings. Circle the word that best completes the sentence.
4.   (Would Wood) you like to meet my friend?

Day 2

Circle the letters that should be capitalized.
1.   byron has a dog named tilly and a cat named wilbur.
If the group of words is a complete sentence, color the fish purple. If the group of words is not a sentence, color the fish green.
2.   at the bottom of the ocean
Add quotation marks around what the person said.
3.   Todd said, I like dogs.
Some words sound alike but have different meanings. Circle the word that best completes the sentence.
4.   Ginny wore a (blew blue) dress.

Day 3

Circle the letters that should be capitalized.
1.   my teacher is mrs. johnson.
If the group of words is a complete sentence, color the fish purple. If the group of words is not a sentence, color the fish green.
2.   The whale lives in the deep water.
Add quotation marks around what the person said.
3.   I'm going to walk to school, said Sue.
Some words sound alike but have different meanings. Circle the word that best completes the sentence.
4.   My brother is (for four) years old.

Day 4

Circle the letters that should be capitalized.
1.   jerry went to wyoming last year for Father's Day.
If the group of words is a complete sentence, color the fish purple. If the group of words is not a sentence, color the fish green.
2.   swims along the rocky shore
Add quotation marks around what the person said.
3.   Hit the ball! Bryan yelled at his little brother.
Some words sound alike but have different meanings. Circle the word that best completes the sentence.
4.   The (sun son) helps plants make food.

Circle the letters that should be capitalized.

1. alicia read *the wind in the willows.*

2. aunt carmon is my favorite aunt.

3. brandon celebrates christmas with his grandparents.

Read each group of words. If the group of words is a complete sentence, color the fish purple. If the group of words is not a sentence, color the fish green.

4. The ocean is very salty.

5. the great white shark

Add quotation marks around what each person said.

6. I love apple pie, Emma told me.

7. You will like this story, Jose said.

Some words sound alike but have different meanings. Circle the word that best completes each sentence.

8. (Wood Would) you like some ice cream?

9. She had bright (blue blew) eyes.

10. I have (for four) new pairs of shoes.

Joshua wants to be an actor more than anything. He takes acting classes. He has been in plays. He has a chance to be in another play. He has to try out this afternoon. The phone rings. Joshua's friend wants him to come over this afternoon.

1. What does Joshua love to do? _____

2. What does Joshua do about the thing he loves: **daydream about doing it** or **take classes and do it**? _____

3. What is Joshua's problem? _____

4. What will Joshua probably do?
A. Joshua will go to his friend's house.   B. Joshua will go to try out for the play.

Day 1

All animals have to eat to stay alive. Squirrels eat nuts. Whales eat sea plants and animals. Other animals eat many different things. A squirrel is hungry. He sees a pile of sea plants and a pile of nuts.

1. If you caught a squirrel, which word with **qu** do you think would best describe the squirrel: **quiet** or **squirmy**? _____

2. What do squirrels eat? _____ What do whales eat? _____

3. What decision does the squirrel have to make? _____

4. Predict what the squirrel will do.
A. The squirrel will eat the nuts.   B. The squirrel will eat the sea plants.

Day 2

Dawn has been racing bikes every day after school for two years. She is tired of bike races. She wants to try something new. Dawn's teacher asks Dawn to swim on the swim team after school.

1. How long has Dawn been racing her bike? _____

2. How does she feel about bike racing now? _____

3. What decision does Dawn have to make? _____

_____

4. What will Dawn probably do?
A. Dawn will swim.   B. Dawn will race on her bike.

Day 3

Lucy has a favorite uncle. She wants to buy him a birthday present. He likes fishing, so she wants to buy him a fishing book. Lucy saves her money for two months. Finally, she has enough money for the book.

1. Whom does Lucy want to buy a present for? _____

2. What does Lucy know about her uncle? _____

3. How long does Lucy save money? _____

4. Predict what Lucy will do with the money.
A. Lucy will buy herself a new game.
B. Lucy will buy a fishing book for her uncle.

Day 4

Boa Constrictors

Boa constrictors are very big. They can grow to be up to 14 feet (4.3 meters) long. Boas are not poisonous. A boa kills its prey by squeezing it. Then, the boa swallows the prey.

Boas do not eat cows or other large animals. They do eat some animals that are larger than their own heads. The bones in their jaws stretch so that they can swallow small animals such as rodents and birds.

Boa constrictors hunt while hanging from trees. They watch for their prey. Then, they attack. After eating, they may sleep for a week. Boas do not need to eat often. They can live without food for many months.

Boa constrictors give birth to live baby snakes. They do not lay eggs. They may have up to 50 baby snakes at one time.

1. What is this passage about?

   _____

2. Does the first paragraph tell you what kind of animal a boa constrictor is? _____
   If so, what? _____

3. The boa is hungry and hunting for food. Which type of prey will it most likely eat?
   A. cow
   B. panther
   C. mouse

4. Baby boa constrictors are born as
   A. hatchlings from an egg.
   B. little, live snakes.
   C. full-grown snakes.

5. Circle the paragraph above where the writer finally tells you what type of animal a boa constrictor is.

Prewrite/Brainstorm

Do you know someone who deserves a "thank-you"? Read the three ideas. Circle one that you like. To begin writing a thank-you letter, list three reasons why you want to say "thank you."

Three Reasons

1. Thank you for the nice gift.

2. Thank you for being so nice.

3. Thank you for thinking of me.

_____

_____

_____

Draft

Write your letter to someone who deserves a "thank-you." Use the format shown here. Be sure that you include the date and the person's name. At the end, sign your letter.

Date:

Dear _____,

_____

_____

_____

_____

Your friend,

Revise

After you write your letter, read it to make sure that it says what you want it to say. Does the letter have the date and a friendly greeting? Did you say "thank you" for something specific? Rewrite your letter with more specific words.

_____

_____

_____

_____

Proofread

Read your letter again. Do you see any capitalization errors? Are all of the words spelled correctly? Did you use the correct punctuation and grammar? Use proofreading marks to correct the sentences.

❑ Capitalization mistakes
❑ Grammar mistakes
❑ Punctuation mistakes
❑ Spelling mistakes

Publish

Write your final copy on a computer or on the lines below.
MAKE SURE it turns out

- NEAT—Make sure there are no wrinkles, creases, or holes.
- CLEAN—Erase any smudges or dirty spots.
- EASY TO READ—Use your best handwriting and good spacing between words.

_____

_____

_____

_____

_____

_____

_____

_____

_____

_____

_____

_____

_____

A long time ago, the sky was very close to the earth. When people were hungry, they just reached up and ate the sky. Sometimes, the sky tasted like beef stew, corn, or pineapple. Everyone was happy because they always had plenty to eat.

1. Which compound word has the **short a** sound in it? _____

2. What is the opposite of **plenty**? _____

3. Did this story really happen, or is it a fantasy? _____

4. According to the story, how did the people of long ago get their food?

    A. They hunted.   B. They grew crops.   C. They ate the sky.

Day 1

People began wasting the sky. They would break off big pieces and throw away the leftovers. The sky became angry.

"Do not waste me. Only break off what you can eat. If you don't take care of me, I will go far away," said the sky.

1. Does the **ow** in **throw** sound like the **ow** in **now** or in **own**? _____

2. When you **waste** something, are you throwing away **something you can use** or **just some garbage**? _____

3. Choose one sentence in the story that you think is the most impossible. Underline it.

4. How does the sky feel? _____

Day 2

For a while, the people were careful not to waste the sky. After a time, the people began to waste the sky again. The sky became angry.

1. Which vowel sound is in **waste** and **became**? short a   long a   long e

2. What does it mean to be **careful**?

    A. to pay attention   B. to be sad   C. to make a law

3. Why do you think the people began to waste the sky again? _____

4. Are you like the people in this story sometimes? _____
    Do you ever forget things you have been told to do or not to do? _____

Day 3

"You are still wasting me. From now on, you will have to hunt and grow your own food!" yelled the sky as he went very far away.

The people were sad. Now, they had to grow and hunt for their food. They learned that it is not a good idea to waste the gifts of nature.

1. Does the **ow** in **grow** sound like the **ow** in **now** or in **own**? _____

2. Which word could you use instead of **yelled**?   A. shouted   B. whispered

3. What is a better title for this story?
    A. The Sky Gets Mad   B. Why the Sky Is Far Away

4. This is a folktale from Nigeria. Folktales have a lesson that is true, even if the story is not. The true lesson in this story is "Do not _____."

Day 4

A Warm Summer Day

(1) "What a beautiful day!" thought Trixie the Tree.

(2) "Hey! Let's go climb the apple tree. We'll see the whole park from the top," said James. "We can also smell the apple blossoms," said Sara.

(3) The children ran over to Trixie the Tree. They began to climb her huge branches.

(4) "Ha, ha, ha!" laughed Trixie the Tree to herself. "That tickles," she thought.

(5) The children climbed way up the tree. They spent the morning watching the other people in the park and whispering stories to each other.

(6) "Ahh!" sighed Trixie the Tree to herself. "I love when the children come out to play during the summer."

1. Does the **ow** in **low** sound like the **ow** in **now** or in **own**? _____

2. What word could you use instead of **blossoms**? _____

3. Which paragraphs could really happen? Circle the numbers below.

   (1)   (2)   (3)   (4)   (5)   (6)

4. What does Trixie the Tree say to herself when the children climb her branches?
   A.   "Ouch, that hurts."
   B.   "Ha, ha, ha! That tickles."
   C.   "I sure hope they don't pick my flowers."

5. Which paragraphs are fantasy? Circle the numbers below.

   (1)   (2)   (3)   (4)   (5)   (6)

2.RL.1, 2.RL.2, 2.RF.3, 2.RF.4, 2.L.3

Day 1

Write **there**, **their**, or **they're** to correctly complete the sentence. Circle each letter that should be capitalized.

1. & 2. it was _____ when i looked.

Use **or**, **and**, or **but** to join the sentences. Use proofreading marks.

3. In his backyard, Juan found a cricket. Juan found a ladybug.

Read the invitation. Place commas in the right places.

4.

It's a birthday party!
Chandra Park
Date: October 9 2014
Place: 423 Center Street
        Bath Maine 89764

Day 2

Write **there**, **their**, or **they're** to correctly complete the sentence. Circle each letter that should be capitalized.

1. & 2. _____ french toast was tasty.

Use **or**, **and**, or **but** to join the sentences. Use proofreading marks.

3. Britney likes math. Britney likes art.

Read the envelope. Place commas in the right places.

4.

Chandra Park
423 Center Street
Bath Maine 89764

Day 3

Write **there**, **their**, or **they're** to correctly complete the sentence. Circle each letter that should be capitalized.

1. & 2. _____ students in mr. hsu's class.

Use **or**, **and**, or **but** to join the sentences. Use proofreading marks.

3. We might have pizza for lunch. We might have salad for lunch.

Read the invitation. Place commas in the right places.

4.

You're invited to a party!
Lin Novak
Date: January 23 2014
Place: 37 West Road
        Tampa Florida 62341

Day 4

Write **there**, **their**, or **they're** to correctly complete the sentence. Circle each letter that should be capitalized.

1. & 2. give _____ tickets to them.

Use **or**, **and**, or **but** to join the sentences. Use proofreading marks.

3. I ran to school. I was late.

Read the envelope. Place commas in the right places.

4.

Lin Novak
37 West Road
Tampa Florida 62341

Write **there**, **their**, or **they're** to correctly complete each sentence. Circle each letter that should be capitalized.

1. & 2. i think _____ riding the roller coaster.

3. & 4. the roller coaster is over _____ by mrs. farmer.

5. & 6. We will go _____ to eat english muffins.

Use **or**, **and**, or **but** to join the sentences. Use proofreading marks.

7. Dennis went to Ann's party. Tony went to Ann's party.

8. I saw you. I did not hear what you said.

Read the invitation and the envelope. Place commas in the right places.

9.

> Boo! It's a Halloween party!
> Tyrone Hansen
> Date: October 31 2015
> Place: My house
>   10024 Wells Avenue
>   Claremont California 91734

10.

> Tyrone Hansen   ☐
> 10024 Wells Avenue
> Claremont California
>   91734

What Would You Expect?

Isabel threw a little rock into a pond. Circles rippled out in the water around the little rock. More and more circles rippled until the ripples reached the shore.

1. Who is in this story? _____

2. Is Isabel a boy or a girl? _____

3. Where does this story happen? _____

4. What will happen if Isabel throws another little rock into the pond?
    A. Circles will ripple out into the water.
    B. An angry frog will yell at Isabel.

Jaime never eats anything sweet. He went to Geneva's party. Geneva served sandwiches, popcorn, ice cream, and birthday cake. Jaime had fun.

1. Who is in this story? _____

2. What do you know about Jaime? _____

3. What kind of party is it? _____

4. What did Jaime eat?
    A. cake and popcorn
    B. sandwiches and popcorn

The rain went on for hours and hours. Puddles formed on the streets. But, the sun finally came out. The temperature rose to more than 100 degrees. The temperature stayed that hot for two days. There was no more rain.

1. What season is it in the story? _____

2. Does the temperature often go above 100 degrees where you live? _____

3. Do you like very hot and sunny weather or rainy weather better? _____

4. What do you think happened after two days in the story?
    A. The puddles were gone.
    B. The puddles were the same size.

Chin loves to count. She counts everything. She counts leaves. She even counts clouds. The math test is tomorrow. Chin practices counting and adding all evening.

1. Who is in this story? _____

2. Is Chin a boy or a girl? _____

3. What does Chin love to do? _____

4. How will Chin do on the test?
    A. Chin will do poorly.
    B. Chin will not take the test.
    C. Chin will do well.

Time for Dusty

Dusty wanted something. He ran to find Tyler. Tyler was reading a book. Dusty walked up the stairs to Holly's bedroom. She was playing a game. She did not look to see what Dusty wanted.

Dusty ran back down the steps. He picked up his leash.

He took the leash and went to Tyler. This time, Tyler put his book down. "What do you want, boy?" Tyler asked.

Dusty ran to the door. He wagged his tail.

Tyler pulled on his coat. He went to the steps and said, "Holly, do you want to go outside with us?"

"Yes," said Holly. She smiled.

1. What is the main idea of this story?

   _____

2. Who are the characters in this story? _____

3. What is Dusty?

   A. a kid

   B. a dog

   C. a cat

4. What does Dusty want to do? _____

   _____

5. Predict what will happen next. _____

   _____

Prewrite/Brainstorm

Some people write stories about their lives. You can too! Fill in the lines to begin your autobiography.

My name is _____.

My favorite toy is _____.

My favorite color is _____.

I like to eat _____.

My friends are _____.

Day 1

Draft

Rewrite your sentences in a paragraph. Make sure you write them in the order you want them to be said.

_____

_____

_____

_____

Day 2

Revise

Read your paragraph about yourself. Did you use all of your ideas? Can you make your sentences clearer? Rewrite the paragraph. Be sure to use specific nouns and verbs.

_____

_____

_____

_____

Day 3

Proofread

Read your paragraph again. Do you see any capitalization errors? Are all of the words spelled correctly? Did you use the correct punctuation and grammar? Use proofreading marks to correct the sentences.

❒ Capitalization mistakes
❒ Grammar mistakes
❒ Punctuation mistakes
❒ Spelling mistakes

Day 4

Publish

Write your final copy on a computer or on the lines below.
MAKE SURE it turns out

- NEAT—Make sure there are no wrinkles, creases, or holes.
- CLEAN—Erase any smudges or dirty spots.
- EASY TO READ—Use your best handwriting and good spacing between words.

_____

_____

_____

_____

_____

_____

_____

_____

_____

_____

_____

_____

_____

Life in the Midwest

Brandy is a second grader who lives in the part of the United States that is known as the Midwest. She lives on a farm in Nebraska.

1. Who is in this story? _____

2. Is this person a boy or a girl? _____

3. What state does he or she live in? _____

4. Which is a better summary of this paragraph: **Nebraska is in the Midwest** or **Brandy is a second grader from a farm in Nebraska**? Underline it.

Day 1

The Midwest is a very fertile part of the United States. This means that the Midwest is a place where it is easy to grow plants.

1. Do you live in the Midwest? _____

2. What does **fertile** mean? _____

3. Why is the Midwest a good place for a farm? _____
   _____

4. Which is a better summary of this paragraph: **The Midwest is a fertile place** or **Fertile places are in the United States**? Underline it.

Day 2

Prairie land is all around Brandy's farm. The prairie is a large open space of land. It is very flat and grassy. Many kinds of animals live on the prairie, such as prairie dogs, coyotes, buffalo, and wild mustangs.

1. Write three words that describe the prairie. _____

2. Are the animals in the prairie **wild** or **tame**? _____

3. Write the name of three animals that live on the prairie. _____

4. Fill in words from the paragraph to complete the summary. Brandy's _____ is surrounded by prairie land that is very _____ and _____. Prairie dogs, _____, _____, and _____ live on the prairie.

Day 3

Brandy enjoys helping on the farm, skating, and learning about science in her small class of only three children.

1. Does Brandy go to school with many other children? _____

2. How many other children are in her class? _____

3. Would you like to live where Brandy does? _____
   Why or why not? _____

4. Write a summary of this paragraph in your own words. _____
   _____

Day 4

A Rabbit Poem

The rabbit is small and fast,
With a short and fluffy tail.
He has long ears that let him hear
Scary animals without fail.

Rabbits love to eat and eat!
They love the green, green grass.
They love to munch on vegetables
In a farmer's garden patch.

1. What kind of writing is this?

    _____

2. What is the poem about? _____

3. Write a sentence to tell what rabbits look like. _____

    _____

4. Why did the author write **eat** and **green** twice? _____

5. What two things do rabbits love to eat? _____

6. Write one sentence to summarize the entire poem. _____

    _____

2.RL.1, 2.RL.4, 2.RL.10, 2.RF.4, 2.L.4

Use proofreading marks to show correct capitalization and punctuation of the sentences.

   1. & 2. lin had a birthday party How many people were at the party

Write **is** or **are** to correctly complete the sentence.

   3.   The children _____ putting on ice skates.

Read the sentence. If **to**, **too**, or **two** is used correctly, color the picture. If the word is used incorrectly, cross out the word and write the correct word below it.

   4.   Gabriel is going too catch the ball.

Use proofreading marks to show correct capitalization and punctuation of the sentences.

   1. & 2. roberto and maria came to the party They live across the street

Write **is** or **are** to correctly complete the sentence.

   3.   Andre _____ already skating.

Read the sentence. If **to**, **too**, or **two** is used correctly, color the picture. If the word is used incorrectly, cross out the word and write the correct word below it.

   4.   It is too windy to go outside.

Use proofreading marks to show correct capitalization and punctuation of the sentences.

   1. & 2. maria gomez gave linda a doll The doll had a yellow hat

Write **is** or **are** to correctly complete the sentence.

   3.   "You _____ skating fast," said the children.

Read the sentence. If **to**, **too**, or **two** is used correctly, color the picture. If the word is used incorrectly, cross out the word and write the correct word below it.

   4.   I see two frogs in the pond.

Use proofreading marks to show correct capitalization and punctuation of the sentences.

   1. & 2. roberto diaz gave her a book What is the book about

Write **is** or **are** to correctly complete the sentence.

   3.   Tia _____ skating too.

Read the sentence. If **to**, **too**, or **two** is used correctly, color the picture. If the word is used incorrectly, cross out the word and write the correct word below it.

   4.   Monkeys love two eat bananas.

Rewrite each sentence with the correct capitalization and punctuation.

1. Did libby have a big birthday cake

   _____

2. john gave his sister warm mittens

   _____

3. Was jamie at the birthday party

   _____

4. libby had a fun party

   _____

Write **is** or **are** to correctly complete each sentence.

5. The children _____ ready.

6. They _____ too.

7. Andy _____ getting tired.

Read each sentence. If **to**, **too**, or **two** is used incorrectly, cross it out and write the correct word above it.

8. To birds sang.

9. Harry went too the zoo.

10. I am going to school.

Mantids

A mantid is an insect. We call it a praying mantis. When it hunts, it lifts its front legs and looks like it is praying.

1. Circle all of the words in the paragraph that have the **short a** sound.

2. What is a **mantid**? _____

3. What is this paragraph mostly about: **the name *praying mantis*** or **how the mantis hunts**? _____

4. Use the information in the paragraph to finish this sentence. A mantid is called a praying mantis because _____.

A mantid can grow to be 2 to 5 inches (5 to 13 centimeters) long. It has front legs with sharp hooks to hold its prey. It has short, wide wings. Its body is long and thin.

1. Does **hooks** rhyme with **books** or with **boots**? _____

2. What is the opposite of **short and wide**? _____

3. What is this paragraph mostly about: **the mantid's front legs** or **what a mantid looks like**? _____

4. Use the information in the paragraph to finish this sentence. A mantid has sharp hooks on its front legs because _____.

Mantids are helpful to people because they eat harmful insects. A female mantid might even eat her mate if she is very hungry.

1. Is the **a** in **mantid** a **long a** or a **short a**? _____

2. What word in this paragraph could be the opposite of **helpful**? _____

3. What is this paragraph mostly about: **what mantids eat** or **the mating habits of the mantid**? _____

4. Use the information in the paragraph to finish this sentence. Mantids eat insects that are harmful to people, but a female mantid will even eat _____.

Mantids protect themselves by changing colors. If a mantid is on a green plant, its color might be green. If it is on a brown branch, its color might be brown.

1. Does **changing** rhyme with **hanging** or **ranging**? _____

2. Which is a word for what the mantid is doing when it changes color to hide itself: **peekaboo** or **camouflage**? _____

3. What is this paragraph mostly about: **how mantids turn green** or **how mantids protect themselves**? _____

4. Use the information in the paragraph to finish this sentence. A mantid protects itself by _____.

Marsupials

A **marsupial** is an animal that has a **pouch**. The pouch is mostly used to **carry babies**. When a baby marsupial is born, the tiny animal must **crawl** into his mother's pouch. There the baby **drinks** his mother's milk and grows. When the baby is big enough to move on his own, he leaves the pouch. The baby stays close to his mother. If in danger, the baby goes back into her pouch.

A **kangaroo**, a **koala**, and an **opossum** are marsupials. These animals do not look alike. They do not eat the same kinds of food, but they all have pouches.

1. Circle each word that has the **short a** sound.

    that   back   animal   baby   danger

    Which word rhymes with **stranger**? _____

2. What is a **marsupial**? _____

3. What is this passage mostly about: **kangaroos** or **the difference between marsupials**?

    _____

4. Name three animals that are marsupials. _____

    _____

5. Use words from the passage to finish this summary.

    The story is about _____. A marsupial is an animal that has a
    _____. The pouch is used mostly to _____.
    When a baby is born, he must _____
    into his mother's pouch. Inside the pouch, the baby _____ and grows.

6. Compare and contrast the marsupial and the mantid described on the previous page.

    _____

    _____

    _____

    _____

2.RI.1, 2.RI.2, 2.RI.4, 2.RI.9, 2.RI.10, 2.RF.3, 2.RF.4, 2.L.3, 2.L.6

Name_____

Week #36

Day 1

Day 2

Day 3

Day 4

Prewrite/Brainstorm

Describing an object is easy if you have a plan. You can make a plan by writing your ideas in an idea web like the one below. Then, write the ideas from the web in the outline.

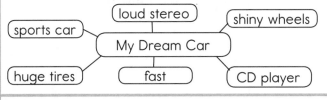

1. topic sentence: It has always been my dream to own a cool sports car.

2. one idea:

3. another idea:

4. last idea:

5. concluding sentence: When I grow up, I will buy a car like this.

Draft

Write sentences about your dream car in a paragraph. Make sure you write them in the order you want them to be said. Keep related ideas together.

_____

_____

_____

_____

Revise

Read your paragraph about your dream car. Did you use all of your ideas? Can you make your sentences clearer? Rewrite the paragraph. Be sure to use specific nouns and verbs.

_____

_____

_____

_____

Proofread

Read your paragraph again. Do you see any capitalization errors? Are all of the words spelled correctly? Did you use the correct punctuation and grammar? Use proofreading marks to correct the sentences.

❐ Capitalization mistakes
❐ Grammar mistakes
❐ Punctuation mistakes
❐ Spelling mistakes

Publish

Write your final copy on a computer or on the lines below.
MAKE SURE it turns out
- NEAT—Make sure there are no wrinkles, creases, or holes.
- CLEAN—Erase any smudges or dirty spots.
- EASY TO READ—Use your best handwriting and good spacing between words.

_____

_____

_____

_____

_____

_____

_____

_____

_____

_____

_____

_____

Chain Reaction

Shannon dropped the marble. It hit the sleeping cat on the nose. The surprised cat jumped on the dog's tail. The dog yipped and chased the cat.

1. What happened first? _____

2. What happened second? _____

3. What happened third? _____

4. What happened fourth? _____

The cat ran under the fish tank. The fish tank wobbled back and forth. Water and one small fish splashed onto the floor. The happy cat ate the fish. The thirsty dog lapped up the water.

1. What was the last effect on the dog? _____

2. What was the last effect on the cat? _____

3. What caused the chain reaction? _____

4. Do you think Shannon dropped the marble on the cat's nose **on purpose** or **by accident**? _____

The Food Chain

Predators are animals that eat other animals. The animals they eat are called prey. Predators and prey do important jobs in nature. Prey animals are food for the animals that hunt them. But, predators also help prey.

1. What do you call an animal that eats other animals? _____

2. What do you call an animal that is eaten by other animals? _____

3. How does the prey help the predator? _____

4. Are people predators or prey? _____

Coyotes hunt rabbits. If coyotes did not eat some rabbits, too many rabbits would be hopping around. There would not be enough food for all of the rabbits to eat. Then, the hungry rabbits would grow weak and sick. Some might even die.

1. Coyotes are called _____ because they eat other animals.

2. Rabbits are called _____ because they are animals that coyotes eat.

3. What would the effect be if coyotes stopped eating rabbits? _____

    _____

4. Does this paragraph tell you what rabbits eat? _____

Day 1

Day 2

Day 3

Day 4

Science Magic

Jeff shared a magic science trick with his class. He said, "How can you tell a raw egg from a hard-boiled egg without cracking it open?"

Marta asked, "Shake it?"

"No," said Jeff. "Watch this. One of these eggs is hard-boiled. The other one is raw."

Jeff placed the eggs on the table. He made each egg spin like a top. Then, he gently touched the top of each egg with two fingers. One egg stopped. The other one kept spinning. Jeff picked up the egg that stopped spinning.

"This is the hard-boiled egg," Jeff said. "The raw egg inside the shell keeps moving. That makes the raw egg keep spinning. The hard-boiled egg stops because nothing inside the shell is moving."

1. What is this story about?

   _____

2. What does Jeff do first? _____

3. How are the two eggs different? _____

4. The raw egg kept moving because _____

   _____ .

5. Why did Jeff do this trick for his class? _____

   _____

Prewrite/Brainstorm

How would your neighborhood be different if a dinosaur lived next door? Use the word web to think of ideas.

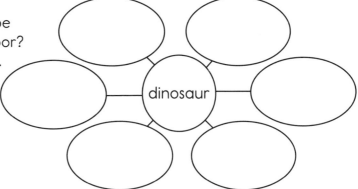

Day 1

Draft

Write two good things and two bad things about a dinosaur living next door. Write four sentences. Use ideas from your word web.

_____

_____

_____

_____

Day 2

Revise

Read your four sentences. Do you want to change the order? Can you make your sentences clearer? Rewrite the sentences. Be sure to use specific nouns and verbs.

_____

_____

_____

_____

Day 3

Proofread

Read your sentences again. Do you see any capitalization errors? Are all of the words spelled correctly? Did you use the correct punctuation and grammar? Use proofreading marks to correct the sentences.

❏ Capitalization mistakes
❏ Grammar mistakes
❏ Punctuation mistakes
❏ Spelling mistakes

Day 4

Publish

Write your final copy on a computer or on the lines below.
MAKE SURE it turns out

- NEAT—Make sure there are no wrinkles, creases, or holes.
- CLEAN—Erase any smudges or dirty spots.
- EASY TO READ—Use your best handwriting and good spacing between words.

_____

_____

_____

_____

_____

_____

_____

_____

_____

_____

_____

_____

Birthdays around the World

Children around the world celebrate their birthdays in many different ways.

In Argentina, people pluck the earlobe of the birthday child. They give one tug for each year the child has been alive.

1. Circle all of the words in the paragraph that have **ck** in them.

2. Which word means the same thing as **tug**: **poke** or **pull**? _____

3. Where is your **earlobe**?   A. top of your ear   B. bottom of your ear

4. How many tugs on your ear would you get on your next birthday? _____

Day 1

People from Nova Scotia have an unusual tradition. Everyone puts butter on the birthday child's nose. They do this so that the child will have good luck. The tradition says that if the child's nose is slippery with butter, bad luck will not stick.

1. Write the words from this paragraph that have **ck** in them. _____

_____

2. What is the opposite of **unusual**: **strange** or **usual**? _____

3. What do people put on the birthday child's nose in Nova Scotia? _____

4. Why do they do that? _____

Day 2

In China, family and friends meet for lunch. They eat noodles to ensure that the child will have a long life.

1. Which words start with **ch**? _____

Which word ends with **ch**? _____

2. What does **ensure** mean: **to figure out** or **to make sure**? _____

3. What time of day do people in China celebrate birthdays? _____

4. Why do they eat noodles for lunch? _____

_____

Day 3

In England, people put objects in the birthday cakes. The birthday child checks her cake. If she finds a coin, it means that she will be rich.

1. Write the word from this paragraph that has **ck** in it. _____

2. What is a **coin**? _____

3. Do you think the birthday child always finds a coin in the cake? _____

4. Look over this week's birthday stories. Which country's birthday celebration would you like to try? _____ Why? _____

_____

Day 4

Jacks and Truyen

Nga moved to the United States from Vietnam when she was in second grade. She met a girl named Denise. Nga and Denise became best friends. They enjoyed many of the same things.

"I want to teach you a game that I used to play with my friends in Vietnam," said Nga. "It is called truyen. You play it with sticks and a piece of fruit. Do you want to try it?"

"Sure," answered Denise. "How do you play?"

"Well, first I lay one stick down. Then, I lay the other sticks across. When I throw this small piece of fruit in the air, I pick up one stick. After that, I throw the fruit up again and pick up two sticks. I keep doing this, and each time I pick up one more stick," explained Nga.

"Hey! I know how to play this game. I call it jacks. At home, I have little metal things called jacks. I bounce a ball and I pick up the jacks one at a time. Then, I pick up two at a time. It's just like truyen!" exclaimed Denise excitedly.

Even though Nga and Denise are from different countries, they still found ways they are alike.

1. Write three words that have **ck** in them. _____

2. What is a **jack**? _____

3. What game did Nga teach Denise: **jacks** or **truyen**? _____

4. How are jacks and truyen the same? _____

   _____

5. How are jacks and truyen different? _____

   _____

Prewrite/Brainstorm

Narrative writing tells a story that may or may not be true. To plan a story, you can use a story map. You need characters, a setting, and a problem. Next, you need events and a solution.

Here are your characters, setting, and problem: You and your best friend are at the beach on Saturday, and you find a bottle with a treasure map inside. You do not know if it is real or not. Write one event and a solution based on this information.

_____

_____

Day 1

Draft

Write a paragraph about you, your friend, and the treasure map you found on the beach. Describe the event that happens after you find the map. Write the solution to the story.

_____

_____

_____

_____

Day 2

Revise

Read your paragraph. Does it tell the story in the right order? Did you introduce your topic? Did you write a solution to the story? Rewrite your paragraph. Be sure to use specific nouns and verbs.

_____

_____

_____

_____

Day 3

Proofread

Read your paragraph again. Do you see any capitalization errors? Are all of the words spelled correctly? Did you use the correct punctuation and grammar? Use proofreading marks to correct the sentences.

❏ Capitalization mistakes
❏ Grammar mistakes
❏ Punctuation mistakes
❏ Spelling mistakes

Day 4

Name_____

Publish

Write your final copy on a computer or on the lines below.

MAKE SURE it turns out

- NEAT—Make sure there are no wrinkles, creases, or holes.
- CLEAN—Erase any smudges or dirty spots.
- EASY TO READ—Use your best handwriting and good spacing between words.

_____

_____

_____

_____

_____

_____

_____

_____

_____

_____

_____

_____

_____

2.W.3, 2.W.5, 2.W.6, 2.W.8, 2.L.1, 2.L.2, 2.L.3

Page 9

Day 1: 1. Answers will vary; 2. Carla; 3. 7; 4. animals and people; **Day 2:** 1. 4; 2. 3; 4. More people live there; 4. Jamie; **Day 3:** 1. the country; 2. her backyard; 3. horses, cows, barns, vegetable gardens, sheep (Answers will vary); 4. horses and cows; **Day 4:** 1. the city; 2. a park; 3. tall buildings, parks, buses, subways, sidewalks (Answers will vary); 4. backyard, animals, garden

Page 10

1. soccer; 2. soccer; 3. A; 4. C; 5. Answers will vary.

Page 11

Day 1: 1. The; 2. (circled) cat, dog; 3. period at end of sentence; 4. birds; **Day 2:** 1. Anne; 2. (circled) hat; 3. period at end of sentence; 4. kittens; **Day 3:** 1. Do; 2. (circled) doll, duck; 3. no period; 4. trees; **Day 4:** 1. Where; 2. (circled) cup; 3. period at end of sentence; 4. gloves

Page 12

1. Fruit; 2. Turn; 3. Blue; 4. (circled) apple, banana; 5. (circled) pig, chicken; 6. (no punctuation); 7. period at end of sentence; 8. period at end of sentence; 9. crayons; 10. eggs

Page 13

Day 1: 1. (circled) each i/I in In, instant, inchworm, inches, In, instant, It, disappear; 2. go away, vanish (Answers will vary); 3. A; 4. short time; **Day 2:** 1. (circled) each o/O in Otter, olives, octagons; 2. B; 3. October; 4. playful; **Day 3:** 1. (circled) each o/O in Oh, overalls, old, bold, Overalls, own, won't; 2. old; 3. new and old; 4. 4; **Day 4:** 1. each u/U in umbrella, up, umbrella, under umbrellas; 2. over; 3. up and down; 4. when it is raining

Page 14

1. soft > short o; funnel > short u; snow > long o; wind > short i; 2. sunshine, thunder; 3. Answers will vary; 4. tornado

Page 15

Day 1: The brainstorming activity should contain various ideas or words related to the topic; **Day 2:** The first draft should contain ideas taken from the brainstorming activity; **Day 3:** The next draft should show improvements in organization and detail of information when compared with the first draft; **Day 4:** The final draft should show proofreading marks where needed.

Page 16

The content of writing samples will vary. Check to be sure that students have correctly completed all of the earlier steps in the writing process and have followed instructions for publishing their work.

Page 17

Day 1: 1. manatees; 2. mammals that live in water; 3. They come to the water's surface; 4. sea cow; **Day 2:** 1. sweet; 2. an animal that eats only plants; 3. calves; 4. mother's milk; **Day 3:** 1. where something lives; 2. Answers will vary; 3. food, water, air, shelter; 4. Yes, their habitat is changing; **Day 4:** 1. pollutants; 2. They get sick; 3. people; 4. Answers will vary.

Page 18

1. warthogs; 2. from the bumps on their faces; 3. tusks, root; 4. thickets, flee; 5. Answers will vary; 6. Answers will vary.

Page 19

Day 1: The brainstorming activity should contain various ideas or words related to the topic; **Day 2:** The first draft should contain ideas taken from the brainstorming activity; **Day 3:** The next draft should show improvements in organization and detail of information when compared with the first draft; **Day 4:** The final draft should show proofreading marks where needed.

Page 20

The content of writing samples will vary. Check to be sure that students have correctly completed all of the earlier steps in the writing process and have followed instructions for publishing their work.

Page 21

Day 1: 1. Marcus; 2. farms; 3. (circled) both; 4. b; **Day 2:** 1. autumn; 2. Answers will vary; 3. bread; 4. a; **Day 3:** 1. poem; 2. Little Miss Muffet; 3. no; 4. (circled) False; **Day 4:** 1. Mary Lou French, Tarantula; 2. poisonous spider; 3. sandwich and chips; 4. (circled) True, She told him to take a long trip.

Page 22

1. Answers will vary; 2. yes; 3. no, He did many experiments; 4. his whole life; 5. (circled) busy, creative, hard-working, musical, smart, talented

Page 23

Day 1: 1. (circled) t, m; 2. (underlined) hides; 3. Answers will vary; 4. glasses; **Day 2:** 1. (circled) t, n; 2. (underlined) eat; 3. Answers will vary; 4. matches; **Day 3:** 1. (circled) s, d, p, w; 2. (underlined) swim; 3. Answers will vary; 4. gases; **Day 4:** 1. (circled) s, t; 2. (underlined) hops; 3. Answers will vary; 4. watches

Page 24

1. (circled) o, s; 2. (circled) w, n, d; 3. (underlined) dances; 4. (underlined) laugh; 5. (underlined) Throw; 6. Answers will vary; 7. Answers will vary; 8. taxes; 9. brushes; 10. switches

Page 25

Day 1: 1. C; 2. A; 3. jealous; 4. that she could be the biggest dog on the block; **Day 2:** 1. (circled) sidewalk, someone, nearby; 2. walked, trotted (Answers will vary); 3. Barker wants to help (Answers will vary); 4. Bruiser; **Day 3:** 1. no; 2. The bushes grabbed him; 3. He is too big to help the boy; 4. Answers will vary; **Day 4:** 1. no; 2. pulled; 3. B; 4. happy (Answers will vary)

Page 26

1. (circled) wrestler, writer; 2. a long spear; 3. C; 4. Answers will vary; 5. She is determined.

Page 27

Day 1: The brainstorming activity should contain various ideas or words related to the topic; **Day 2:** The first draft should contain ideas taken from the brainstorming activity; **Day 3:** The next draft should show improvements in organization and detail of information when compared with the first draft; **Day 4:** The final draft should show proofreading marks where needed.

Page 28

The content of writing samples will vary. Check to be sure that students have correctly completed all of the earlier steps in the writing process and have followed instructions for publishing their work.

Page 29

Day 1: 1. in a mouse house; 2. at midnight; 3. mice; 4. No, their ideas are impossible; **Day 2:** 1. at school; 2. in the morning; 3. Juan, Dylan, their teacher; 4. Answers will vary; **Day 3:** 1. in space; 2. 3010; 3. to the moon; 4. Answers will vary; **Day 4:** 1. in a tree; 2. in the autumn; 3. (circled) squirrel; 4. the nut he hid yesterday

Page 30

1. Grandma's kitchen; 2. It is the kitchen of Maggie's grandma's house; 3. curtains with dots; 4. magnets and Grandma when she bakes; 5. Answers will vary.

Page 31

Day 1: The brainstorming activity should contain various ideas or words related to the topic; **Day 2:** The first draft should contain ideas taken from the brainstorming activity; **Day 3:** The next draft should show improvements in organization and detail of information when compared with the first draft; **Day 4:** The final draft should show proofreading marks where needed.

Page 32

The content of writing samples will vary. Check to be sure that students have correctly completed all of the earlier steps in the writing process and have followed instructions for publishing their work.

Page 33

Day 1: 1. morning; 2. in Lamar's house; 3. Lamar and his mom are about to go on vacation; 4. no; **Day 2:** 1. sunset; 2. at a lake; 3. Answers will vary; 4. no; **Day 3:** 1. 4:00; 2. A; 3. in a submarine deep in the ocean; 4. octopus/animals of the deep ocean; **Day 4:** 1. middle of the night; 2. on top of a mountain; 3. Sasha will go down the mountain; 4. It is cold at night.

Page 34

1. No, it is about work; 2. at the zoo; 3. B; 4. They hide the animals' food; 5. Yes or no; Answers will vary.

Page 35

Day 1: 1. (circled) w, b; 2. P, C; 3. ending period; 4. ate; **Day 2:** 1. (circled) m, a, a; 2. P, P; 3. ending question mark; 4. cane; **Day 3:** 1. (circled) m, g, l; 2. P, C; 3. ending period; 4. kite; **Day 4:** 1. (circled) c, s; 2. C, P; 3. ending period; 4. care

Page 36

1. (circled) u, f; 2. (circled) p, e; 3. (circled) m, j, f; 4. P; 5. C; 6. C; 7. ending exclamation point; 8. ending question mark; 9. Ripe; 10. note

Page 37

Day 1: 1. yes; 2. move it back and forth; 3. a lot; 4. (circled) False; **Day 2:** 1. sung; 2. not possible, cannot happen; 3. Trisha's tooth is getting really loose; 4. Answers will vary; **Day 3:** 1. I, tonight; 2. spit it out; 3. how Trisha's tooth came out; 4. Answers will vary; **Day 4:** 1. **i** in nice; 2. bright (Answers will vary); 3. what the tooth fairy left for Trisha; 4. No, she will not get much money for her teeth.

Page 38

1. (circled) gift, think, slipper; 2. mice; 3. A; 4. Venezuela, Spain; 5. (circled) False

Page 39

Day 1: The brainstorming activity should contain various ideas or words related to the topic; **Day 2:** The first draft should contain ideas taken from the brainstorming activity; **Day 3:** The next draft should show improvements in organization and detail of information when compared with the first draft; **Day 4:** The final draft should show proofreading marks where needed.

Page 40

The content of writing samples will vary. Check to be sure that students have correctly completed all of the earlier steps in the writing process and have followed instructions for publishing their work.

Page 41

Day 1: 1. A; 2. no; 3. Many animals migrate; 4. Answers will vary; **Day 2:** 1. no; 2. not enough food; 3. Birds migrate south so that they can find food; 4. Answers will vary; **Day 3:** 1. no; 2. winter; 3. Some whales migrate to warm waters to raise their young; 4. Answers will vary; **Day 4:** 1. shrimp, squid, small fish; 2. their home stream; 3. Salmon migrate from fresh water to the ocean; 4. Answers will vary.

Page 42

1. Muscles help us move (Answers will vary); 2. Muscles lift, push, and pull. Muscles work at night too; 3. Most movements use voluntary muscles. The brain controls voluntary muscles (Answers will vary); 4. (underlined) Involuntary muscles work without you thinking about them; 5. involuntary

Page 43

Day 1: The brainstorming activity should contain various ideas or words related to the topic; **Day 2:** The first draft should contain ideas taken from the brainstorming activity; **Day 3:** The next draft should show improvements in organization and detail of information when compared with the first draft; **Day 4:** The final draft should show proofreading marks where needed.

Page 44

The content of writing samples will vary. Check to be sure that students have correctly completed all of the earlier steps in the writing process and have followed instructions for publishing their work.

Page 45

Day 1: 1. Ellen and Ava; 2. B; 3. scared, frightened; 4. a noise; **Day 2:** 1. A; 2. in a tent; 3. scream; 4. Answers will vary; **Day 3:** 1. Ava's mother; 2. B; 3. worried about the girls; 4. yes (Answers will vary); **Day 4:** 1. Ava and Ellen slept in the house; 2. Answers will vary; 3. A; 4. Answers will vary

Page 46

1. a grasshopper and an ant; 2. on a hot summer day; 3. B; 4. You should have stored food when food was plenty; 5. C

Page 47

Day 1: 1. "Mary Had a Little Lamb"; 2. (circled) will, (underlined) sing; 3. commas after roses, daisies; 4. You're; **Day 2:** 1. *The Biography of Helen Keller*; 2. (circled) will, (underlined) teach; 3. no commas; 4. your; **Day 3:** 1. *Horse Lover Magazine*; 2. (circled) can, (underlined) come; 3. commas after maple, pine, oak; 4. You're; **Day 4:** 1. *Green Eggs and Ham*; 2. (circled) can, (underlined) watch; 3. commas after math, history; 4. Your

Page 48

1. "Twinkle, Twinkle, Little Star"; 2. *The Big Book of Lizards*; 3. (circled) will, (underlined) write; 4. (circled) can, (underlined) fly; 5. (circled) will, (underlined) rise; 6. commas after Claire, Phil, Taneshia, Joey; 7. commas after blanket, food, drinks; 8. commas after yellow, purple, blue; 9. your; 10. You're

Page 49

Day 1: 1. A; 2. B; 3. cat and mice; 4. They are too busy running from the cat; **Day 2:** 1. know; 2. do not; 3. 4; 4. no; **Day 3:** 1. It is a silent letter; 2. let us; 3. the smallest mouse; 4. to hang a bell around the cat's neck; **Day 4:** 1. B; 2. no; 3. no; 4. They need to get close to the cat to put the bell on.

Page 50

1. (circled) go, no, know, know; 2. (circled) vanished, disappeared, missing; 3. Maria and her pet, Henry; 4. She cannot find Henry; 5. She finds Henry in her shoe.

Page 51

Day 1: The brainstorming activity should contain various ideas or words related to the topic; **Day 2:** The first draft should contain ideas taken from the brainstorming activity; **Day 3:** The next draft should show improvements in organization and detail of information when compared with the first draft; **Day 4:** The final draft should show proofreading marks where needed.

Page 52

The content of writing samples will vary. Check to be sure that students have correctly completed all of the earlier steps in the writing process and have followed instructions for publishing their work.

Page 53

Day 1: 1. fawn; 2. kitten; 3. kid, child, baby; 4. Answers will vary; **Day 2:** 1. 4; 2. elephant, whale, giraffe, cow; 3. elephant, whale, giraffe; 4. cow; **Day 3:** 1. 4; 2. lion, bear, tiger, fox; 3. all of them; 4. lion, tiger; **Day 4:** 1. 3; 2. horse, zebra, donkey; 3. zebra; 4. Answers will vary.

Page 54

1. Answers will vary; 2. (circled) group, sort; 3. (circled) hat, shirt, mitten, shoe, shorts, sock; 4. Things I Play With: truck, ball, doll, paints, book, teddy bear. Things I Wear: hat, sock, mitten, shirt, shoe, shorts; 5. Answers will vary.

Page 55

Day 1: The brainstorming activity should contain various ideas or words related to the topic; **Day 2:** The first draft should contain ideas taken from the brainstorming activity; **Day 3:** The next draft should show improvements in organization and detail of information when compared with the first draft; **Day 4:** The final draft should show proofreading marks where needed.

Page 56

The content of writing samples will vary. Check to be sure that students have correctly completed all of the earlier steps in the writing process and have followed instructions for publishing their work.

Page 57

Day 1: 1. (circled) grew, flew; 2. B; 3. no; 4. (underlined) All of a sudden, wings grew on her back. She flew all the way to the field; **Day 2:** 1. no; 2. A; 3. yes; 4. (nothing underlined); **Day 3:** 1. grandfather, stereos, stereos; 2. ~~gift~~, present; 3. yes; 4. (nothing underlined); **Day 4:** 1. stars, stairs, starry, staircase; starry, staircase; 2. ~~walked~~; Answers will vary; 3. no; 4. (underlined) Michelle pulled stars from the sky. She made stairs from the stars. She walked all of the way up her starry staircase to Mars.

Page 58

1. gorilla, gorillas, understood, Patterson, scientist, together; understood; 2; people; 3. sign language; 4. Koko; 5. Answers will vary.

Page 59

Day 1: 1. (circled) m, i, b, c, s; 2. purple fish; 3. "Jill won a medal,"; 4. (circled) Would; **Day 2:** 1. (circled) b, t, w; 2. green fish; 3. "I like dogs."; 4. (circled) blue; **Day 3:** 1. (circled) m, m, j; 2. purple fish; 3. "I'm going to walk to school,"; 4. (circled) four; **Day 4:** 1. (circled) j, w; 2. green fish; 3. "Hit the ball!"; 4. (circled) sun

Page 60

1. (circled) a, t, w, w; 2. (circled) a, c; 3. (circled) b, c; 4. purple fish; 5. green fish; 6. "I love apple pie,"; 7. "You will like this story,"; 8. (circled) Would; 9. (circled) blue; 10. (circled) four

Page 61

Day 1: 1. act (Answers will vary); 2. take classes and do it; 3. His friend wants to play at the same time as tryouts; 4. B; **Day 2:** 1. squirmy; 2. nuts, sea plants and animals; 3. which pile of food to eat; 4. A; **Day 3:** 1. two years; 2. She is tired of it; 3. to change from bike racing to swimming; 4. B; **Day 4:** 1. her favorite uncle; 2. He likes fishing; 3. two months; 4. A (Answers will vary)

Page 62

1. boa constrictors; 2. no; 3. C; 4. B; 5. (circled) Boa constrictors give birth to live baby snakes. They do not lay eggs. They may have up to 50 baby snakes at one time.

Page 63

Day 1: The brainstorming activity should contain various ideas or words related to the topic; **Day 2:** The first draft should contain ideas taken from the brainstorming activity; **Day 3:** The next draft should show improvements in organization and detail of information when compared with the first draft; **Day 4:** The final draft should show proofreading marks where needed.

Page 64

The content of writing samples will vary. Check to be sure that students have correctly completed all of the earlier steps in the writing process and have followed instructions for publishing their work.

Page 65

Day 1: 1. pineapple; 2. none (Answers will vary); 3. fantasy; 4. C; **Day 2:** 1. own; 2. something you can use; 3. Answers will vary; 4. angry; **Day 3:** 1. (circled) long a; 2. A; 3. They forgot (Answers will vary); 4. yes, Answers will vary; **Day 4:** 1. own; 2. A; 3. B; 4. waste nature's gifts

Page 66

1. own; 2. flowers; 3. (circled) 2, 3, 5; 4. B; 5. 1, 4, 6

Page 67

Day 1: 1. & 2. (circled) i, i; there; 3. In his backyard, Juan found a cricket and a ladybug; 4. commas after 9, Bath; **Day 2:** 1. & 2. (circled) f; Their; 3. Britney likes math and art; 4. comma after Bath; **Day 3:** 1. & 2. (circled) m, h; They're; 3. We might have pizza or salad for lunch; 4. commas after 23, Tampa; **Day 4:** 1. & 2. (circled) g; their; 3. I ran to school but I was late; 4. comma after Tampa

Page 68

1. & 2. (circled) i; they're; 3. & 4. (circled) t, m, f; their; 5. & 6. (circled) e; there; 7. Dennis and Tony went to Ann's party; 8. I saw you but I did not hear what you said; 9. commas after 31, Claremont; 10. comma after Claremont

Page 69

Day 1: 1. Isabel; 2. girl; 3. by a pond; 4. A; **Day 2:** 1. Jaime and Geneva; 2. He does not eat sweet food; 3. birthday party; 4. B; **Day 3:** 1. summer; 2. Answers will vary; 3. Answers will vary; 4. A; **Day 4:** 1. Chin; 2. girl; 3. count; 4. C

Page 70

1. Answers will vary; 2. Dusty, Tyler, Holly; 3. B; 4. Dusty wants to be taken for a walk; 5. Answers will vary.

Page 71

Day 1: The brainstorming activity should contain various ideas or words related to the topic; **Day 2:** The first draft should contain ideas taken from the brainstorming activity; **Day 3:** The next draft should show improvements in organization and detail of information when compared with the first draft; **Day 4:** The final draft should show proofreading marks where needed.

Page 72

The content of writing samples will vary. Check to be sure that students have correctly completed all of the earlier steps in the writing process and have followed instructions for publishing their work.

Page 73

Day 1: 1. Brandy; 2. girl; 3. Nebraska; 4. (underlined) Brandy is a second grader from a farm in Nebraska; **Day 2:** 1. Answers will vary; 2. Plants are easy to grow; 3. It is easy to grow plants in the Midwest; 4. (underlined) The Midwest is a fertile place; **Day 3:** 1. large, flat, grassy (Answers will vary); 2. wild; 3. prairie dogs, coyotes, buffalo (Answers will vary); 4. farm, flat, grassy, coyotes, buffalo, wild mustangs; **Day 4:** 1. no; 2. 2; 3. Answers will vary; 4. Answers will vary.

Page 74

1. a poem; 2. a rabbit; 3. Rabbits are small animals with short fluffy tails and long ears (Answers will vary); 4. It helps the poem's rhythm (Answers will vary); 5. grass and vegetables; 6. Rabbits are small animals that eat grass and vegetables (Answers will vary).

Page 75

Day 1: 1. & 2. (capitalized) lin; period after party, question mark after party; 3. are; 4. too to; **Day 2:** 1. & 2. (capitalized) roberto, maria; periods after party, street; 3. is; 4. color picture; **Day 3:** 1. & 2. (capitalized) Maria, Gomez, Linda; periods after doll, hat; 3. are; 4. color picture; **Day 4:** 1. & 2. (capitalized) roberto, diaz; period after book; question mark after about; 3. is; 4. two to

Page 76

1. Did Libby have a big birthday cake?; 2. John gave his sister warm mittens.; 3. Was Jamie at the birthday party?; 4. Libby had a fun party.; 5. are; 6. are; 7. is; 8. To Two; 9. too to; 10. correct

Page 77

Day 1: 1. (circled) mantid, mantis, and; 2. an insect; 3. the name *praying mantis*; 4. It looks like it is praying when it hunts; **Day 2:** 1. books; 2. long and thin; 3. what a mantid looks like; 4. It needs them to hold its prey; **Day 3:** 1. short a; 2. harmful; 3. what mantids eat; 4. another mantid; **Day 4:** 1. ranging; 2. camouflage; 3. how mantids protect themselves; 4. changing colors

Page 78

1. (circled) that, back, animal, danger; 2. an animal that has a pouch; 3. the difference between marsupials; 4. kangaroo, koala, opossum; 5; marsupials, pouch, carry babies, crawl, drinks; 6. Answers will vary.

Page 79

Day 1: The brainstorming activity should contain various ideas or words related to the topic; **Day 2:** The first draft should contain ideas taken from the brainstorming activity; **Day 3:** The next draft should show improvements in organization and detail of information when compared with the first draft; **Day 4:** The final draft should show proofreading marks where needed.

Page 80

The content of writing samples will vary. Check to be sure that students have correctly completed all of the earlier steps in the writing process and have followed instructions for publishing their work.

Page 81

Day 1: 1. Shannon dropped the marble; 2. The marble hit the cat on the nose; 3. The cat jumped on the dog's tail; 4. The dog chased the cat; **Day 2:** 1. The dog drank water; 2. The cat ate a fish; 3. Shannon dropped a marble; 4. by accident (Answers will vary); **Day 3:** 1. predator; 2. prey; 3. It is food for the predator; 4. predators; **Day 4:** 1. predators; 2. prey; 3. Too many rabbits for their food, and some would die; 4. no

Page 82

1. Answers will vary; 2. Jeff asks the class a question; 3. One is hard-boiled and the other one is raw; 4. The egg inside the shell keeps moving; 5. Answers will vary.

Page 83

Day 1: The brainstorming activity should contain various ideas or words related to the topic; **Day 2:** The first draft should contain ideas taken from the brainstorming activity; **Day 3:** The next draft should show improvements in organization and detail of information when compared with the first draft; **Day 4:** The final draft should show proofreading marks where needed.

Page 84

The content of writing samples will vary. Check to be sure that students have correctly completed all of the earlier steps in the writing process and have followed instructions for publishing their work.

Page 85

Day 1: 1. (circled) pluck; 2. pull; 3. B; 4. Answers will vary; **Day 2:** 1. luck, luck, stick; 2. usual; 3. butter; 4. so the child will have good luck; **Day 3:** 1. China, child, lunch; 2. to make sure; 3. lunchtime; 4. to ensure that the child will have a long life; **Day 4:** 1. checks; 2. money; 3. Answers will vary; 4. Answers will vary.

Page 86

1. sticks, jacks, pick (Answers will vary); 2. a little metal thing used in jacks; 3. truyen; 4. You pick up something from the ground before you catch something else; 5. truyen uses sticks, and fruit is thrown; jacks uses metal things, and a ball is bounced.

Page 87

Day 1: The brainstorming activity should contain various ideas or words related to the topic; **Day 2:** The first draft should contain ideas taken from the brainstorming activity; **Day 3:** The next draft should show improvements in organization and detail of information when compared with the first draft; **Day 4:** The final draft should show proofreading marks where needed.

Page 88

The content of writing samples will vary. Check to be sure that students have correctly completed all of the earlier steps in the writing process and have followed instructions for publishing their work.